**Risk,
Return,
and
Equilibrium**

A General
Single-Period
Theory
of Asset
Selection
and
Capital-Market
Equilibrium

The MIT Press
Cambridge,
Massachusetts,
and London,
England

**Risk**
**Return**
**and**
**Equilibrium**

A General
Single-Period
Theory
of Asset
Selection
and
Capital-Market
Equilibrium

Bernell
Kenneth
Stone

Set in Monophoto
Times Roman
Printed and bound
in the United States
of America by The
Colonial Press Inc.

ISBN 0 262 19071 0
(hardcover)

Library of Congress
catalog card
number: 79-113728

# Preface

This book is based on a doctoral dissertation submitted to the Sloan School of Management of the Massachusetts Institute of Technology in the latter part of 1968. It contains most of the results of that document with some revisions, extensions, and editorial changes.

This volume emphasizes clarity of presentation at the graduate level. Although considerable use is made of mathematics, great care has been taken to present proofs and derivations in sufficient detail to make them easy to follow. The level of the mathematics is not advanced. It is hoped that the book will find use as collateral reading in graduate courses in economics and finance, as a text in advanced finance courses dealing with risk, asset selection, or capital markets, and as a reference for professionals in the field.

I appreciate the comments, suggestions, and criticisms of my dissertation committee, Professors Paul Cootner, Franco Modigliani, and Stewart Myers. Professor Cootner in particular has been a most helpful advisor; my association with him has been extremely valuable to me. His availability, suggestions, comments, criticisms, editorial contributions, and encouragement have been invaluable.

The comments and suggestions of Professors Modigliani and Myers were also helpful. In particular, the opportunity afforded by Professor Modigliani to present major portions of my work to the Sloan School finance seminar was quite beneficial. Professor Modigliani's comments and questions at this time were much appreciated and contributed significantly to my work. I also benefited from the questions and suggestions of my fellow graduate students and Professors Myers, Scholes, Pogue, and Farrar. Frequent discussions with David Pyle and Daniel Rie were also valuable. The comments of Daniel Rie have been especially valuable in converting the dissertation into this book.

In preparing the manuscript for publication, I have obtained comments from Professor John W. Pratt on Chapter 3. I am indebted to the pioneering works of Sharpe, Littner, and Mossin upon which I have built.

Finally, I thank my wife, Sandy, for her encouragement, for providing a pleasant work environment, and for conscientiously typing and editing many drafts. No perfunctory uxorial acknowledgment can convey how much her help and encouragement have contributed to this work.

My studies at the Sloan School were financed in part by a National Defense Education Act Fellowship. I am grateful for this support and for the excellent academic environment provided by the Sloan School.

Despite these acknowledgments of help gratefully received, it bears stating that I accept full responsibility for the resulting volume, including those errors which may remain.

B.K.S.

# Figures

**Tables**

**Risk,**
**Return,**
**and**
**Equilibrium**

A General
Single-Period
Theory
of Asset
Selection
and
Capital Market
Equilibrium

# 1
## Overview

The role of uncertainty in financial decision-making has been the predominant concern of contemporary financial theory. A number of measures of risk have been adduced, and at least three conceptual frameworks have been developed to treat the effects of uncertainty. These frameworks are the homogeneous risk-class concept of Modigliani and Miller, the Markowitz mean-variance criterion for portfolio analysis, and the time-state-preference model. The risk-class concept is designed to treat decision-making without requiring a general equilibrium model. The time-state-preference framework is a very general treatment of uncertainty in the context of market equilibrium; however, the abstract framework of the time-state-preference models are such that it is difficult to extract specific implications from the model.

The Markowitz mean-variance criterion has been widely used in portfolio selection; it has also been the basis of mean-variance capital-market equilibrium models developed by Sharpe [26], Lintner [15, 16], and Mossin [19].

The mean-variance models are less abstract than the time-state-preference models in assuming a particular measure of risk (variance) and a utility function that depends on only two parameters (mean and variance). Among the specific issues that have been raised in the mean-variance market equilibrium models are (1) Given that variance is the measure of portfolio risk, what is the proper measure of security risk? (2) For a measure of security risk, what is the relation between expected return on a security and its risk? (3) What is the relation between portfolio return and portfolio risk at market equilibrium, and is this relation linear?

Of course, the answer to the question of what is the proper measure of security risk is highly dependent on the measure of portfolio risk. Likewise, the relation between security return and security risk or between portfolio return and portfolio risk depends on what one uses as the measure of risk. Although these questions have been asked with variance or standard deviation as the measure of risk, there has been no market equilibrium model that has asked the same questions in the context of a general measure of risk. One reason for the lack of a general treatment is that no general measures of portfolio risk have been developed.[1]

In the literature variance has been the most pervasive measure of risk; its validity or lack of validity as a risk measure has been discussed extensively. It is widely recognized that a quadratic utility function is sufficient to justify the mean-variance criterion. Tobin [28] asserted that the security returns being distributed according to a two-parameter probability distribution is sufficient

---

[1] One possible exception to this statement is the risk premium (Cf. Pratt [22]). The risk premium as a risk measure for portfolios will be considered in Chapter 3.

to establish the dependence of the expected utility on mean and variance alone. However, Fama [5] showed that Tobin's derivation also required that the two-parameter distribution possess the property of finite additivity.[2] Fama [5] and Samuelson [24] have focused on the Paretian family of distributions and considered other measures of dispersion of the probability distribution.

Other special measures of risk have also been used, including loss functions, chance constraints, and confidence limits. These measures have been less intensively studied than variance in the theoretical literature, and none have yet been employed in market equilibrium models.

Although the use of two-parameter utility functions contributes greatly to the conceptual and analytical treatability of the Sharpe, Lintner, and Mossin models, there has been no serious effort to extend the basic structure of the model to a general two-parameter utility function that depends on some general measure of risk. No one has attempted to answer in a general context the questions asked in the mean-variance formulations. Moreover, even within the existing mean-variance formulations, there has been neither a critical evaluation of the role played by the simplifying assumptions nor a conscientious, systematic attempt to remove the simplifying assumptions.

This work attempts to develop a general measure of portfolio risk and to formulate a general model of asset selection in the context of market equilibrium. The major concern is the definition and elucidation of theoretical issues; the emphasis is on the logical structure of the arguments and the role of the assumptions in obtaining results. Arguments are quantitatively formulated.

In Chapter 2 relevant aspects of the Markowitz theory of portfolio selection are summarized, and a brief overview of the Sharpe, Lintner, and Mossin models is presented.

Chapter 3 deals with the issue of measures of risk and the formulation of two-parameter utility functions. A global measure of risk is defined and investigated. Two alternative formulations of expected utility in terms of return and risk are presented.

In Chapter 4 the notation is summarized; the assumptions of the model are stated and discussed; the general structure of the model is analyzed.

Chapter 5 is a thorough investigation of asset selection and market equilibrium for a general two-parameter representation of expected utility. In this chapter first-order conditions are derived, general theorems are stated and then more specific results obtained as additional assumptions are added

---

[2] A class of distributions $C$ is said to be finitely additive if and only if a linear combination of elements of class $C$ also belongs to $C$. The normal distribution is an example of a finitely additive class of distributions.

to the model. Issues treated include (1) How are portfolio risk and portfolio return related? Under what conditions can a solution for return as a function of risk be obtained and under what conditions will the relation be linear? (2) What measure of security risk is implied by a measure of portfolio risk and what is the relation between security return and security risk? (3) How do individual investor's preferences and (differing) expectations interact to determine security prices for any given supply of securities? (4) What effect does the existence of a riskless asset have on portfolio selection? The role of homogeneity of the risk function is considered and shown to result in important simplifications.

Chapter 6 is a brief specialization of Chapter 5 to the general risk measures developed in Chapter 3. It contains examples of these risk measures for special utility functions.

In Chapters 7 and 8 the general results of the preceding chapters are specialized to mean-variance models. The major results of and important extensions to the Sharpe, Lintner, and Mossin models are derived; special attention is paid to the role of the assumptions. The relation between the models is investigated.

Some effort has been made to make the chapters as self-contained as possible. Chapter 3 is completely self-contained. Chapters 7 and 8 can be read as self-contained units dealing with the Sharpe, Lintner, and Mossin models, although reading Chapter 5 enhances these chapters considerably. Chapter 5 requires major portions of Chapters 3 and 4; Chapter 6 requires Chapters 3, 4, and 5. Chapter 2 is simply a review of previous work.

The following symbols are used in the book.

| Symbol | Meaning |
|--------|---------|
| $\Rightarrow$ | implies |
| $\Leftrightarrow$ | is equivalent to |
| $\doteq$ | is approximately equal to |
| $\in$ | belongs to or is a member of |
| $\notin$ | does not belong to |
| $H^k$ | the class of functions that is homogeneous of degree $k$ |

Vectors will be printed in **boldface** type, matrices in sans serif type for Latin letters and lightface type for Greek letters. Notation in Chapters 2 and 3 is defined and developed as needed; Section 4.1 gives a summary of the variable definitions and other notation. Section 5.1 and Lemma 5.3 summarize some frequently used variable transformations.

# 2
# Mean-Variance
# Market-
# Equilibrium
# Models

## 2.1. The Markowitz Asset-Selection Model

The modern history of normative asset selection under conditions of risk begins with the publication of "Portfolio Selection" in the 1952 *Journal of Finance* by Harry Markowitz [17]. In his paper, Markowitz assumes that (1) Investors have (or can form) probability distributions about the future performance of securities. (2) These distributions have finite means and variances. (3) There are decreasing returns to risk bearing beyond some point. (4) An individual's preferences are a function of mean portfolio return and variance only. (5) For any given expected return on a portfolio, the portfolio with the smallest variance is preferred to all others; for any given portfolio variance, the portfolio with maximum expected return is preferred to all others.

Markowitz called Assumption 5 the *mean-variance (M-V) criterion*. This assumption was the significant innovation of Markowitz that reduced portfolio selection to a quadratic programing problem.

The quadratic programing problem is to minimize the quadratic form $V = \mathbf{y}' \cdot \Sigma \cdot \mathbf{y}$ for any given level of return $\rho = \mathbf{y}' \cdot \mathbf{r}$, where $V$ is the portfolio variance, $\rho$ is the portfolio return, $\mathbf{y}$ is the vector of relative investment in each security, $\Sigma$ is the covariance matrix, and $\mathbf{r}$ is the vector of expected returns.[1] Markowitz called the solution to this problem an efficient portfolio and the collection of all possible solutions was called an *efficient frontier*.[2] The efficient frontier $EF$ and set of utility indifference curves $U_1$, $U_2$, and $U_3$ are sketched in Figure 2.1. The curve $EF$ is drawn for the case in which there is no riskless asset. If there is a riskless asset, the new efficient frontier (indicated by $E'F'$) will be tangent to $EF$ intersecting the $\rho$ axis at the riskless rate $r_n$. The points $P$ and $P'$ are the optimal portfolios in the case of no riskless asset and a riskless asset, respectively.

To summarize, the Markowitz procedure reduced the portfolio selection problem to one of measurement, calculation, and final selection. The measurement involved the formation of expectations regarding the mean return, its variance, and its covariance; the calculation required the solution of a parametric quadratic programing problem; the selection involved choosing

[1] Other constraints can, of course, be added; e.g., that $\mathbf{y} > \mathbf{O}$.
[2] The fact that a set of solutions must be generated means that the problem is really a parametric quadratic programing problem. This can be formulated as $\min(\mathbf{y}' \cdot \Sigma \cdot y - \theta y' \cdot r)$, where $\theta$ is a parameter to be varied. This formulation of the parametric programing problem was presented by Wolf [31]. A very readable discussion of it is contained in Hadley [10], Chapter 7, especially Section 5.

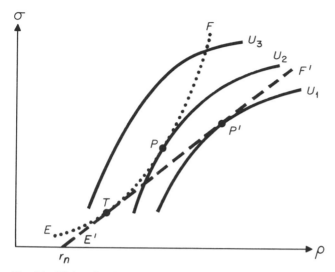

Fig. 2.1. Efficient frontier and indifference curves. Key: ······· = $EF$ = efficient frontier with no riskless asset; - - - - - = $E'F'$ = efficient frontier with a riskless asset; ——— = $U_3, U_2, U_1$ = isoutility lines.

that point on the efficient frontier that maximized the individual's utility function.

## 2.2. Portfolio-Selection Models of Market Equilibrium[3]

In the Markowitz framework, demand for securities is a derived demand. Securities are not sought for their properties per se, but rather for their ability to produce desired properties in a security portfolio. The Markowitz asset-selection procedure is formulated within a comparative statics framework in which prices are taken as given. The model may, however, be generalized from a model of asset selection alone to a theory of asset-market equilibrium. In generalizing the mean-variance portfolio selection procedures to a model of asset-market equilibrium, it is assumed that all individuals in the market are utility maximizing M-V portfolio selectors, and it is required that prices be such that markets are cleared.

[3] In this analysis we are restricting the evaluation to the capital market equilibrium models that are characterized by a risk-return formulation of the portfolio selection problem. Another type of model which has not explicitly focused on the risk-return issue but which has formulated a model of security selection based on utility maximization are time-state-preference models. This type of model was first introduced by Arrow [2] and developed further by Hirshliefer [12, 13, 14]. Recent papers have also been written by Myers [21] and Diamond [4]. Although the models are conceptually different, there is some overlap in both assumptions and issues broached. We shall restrict our analysis to the risk-return type of formulation presented by Sharpe, Lintner, and Mossin. Because of the conceptual difference in the models, we shall not include the time-state-preference models in the summary of existing work.

TABLE 2.1. MEAN-VARIANCE MARKET EQUILIBRIUM MODELS.

| Author | Date | Paper |
|--------|------|-------|
| Sharpe | 9/64 | "Capital Asset Prices: A Theory of Market Equilibrium Under Conditions of Risk" (*Journal of Finance*) |
| Lintner | 2/65 | "The Valuation of Risk Assets and the Selection of Risky Investments in Stock Portfolios and Capital Budgets" (*Review of Economics and Statistics*) |
| Lintner | 12/65 | "Security Prices, Risk, and Maximal Gains from Diversification" (*Journal of Finance*) |
| Sharpe | 12/66 | "Security Prices, Risk, and Maximal Gains from Diversification: Reply" (*Journal of Finance*) |
| Mossin | 10/66 | "Equilibrium in a Capital Asset Market" (*Econometrica*) |
| Fama | 2/68 | "Risk, Return and Equilibrium: Some Clarifying Comments" (*Journal of Finance*) |

Market equilibrium models in the M-V portfolio selection tradition have been formulated by Sharpe [27], Lintner [15, 16], and Mossin [19]. Fama [6] has clarified the relation petween the Sharpe and Lintner models and refined the Sharpe treatment. Table 2.1 lists the papers in the portfolio selection tradition of market equilibrium with which this book deals in considerable detail.

The basic structure of the Sharpe, Lintner, and Mossin models is similar. Each postulates a collection of M-V portfolio selectors whose only interaction is reaction to prices and which assumes (1) a single uniform time horizon for all investors; (2) complete agreement about security parameters;[4] (3) the existence of a riskless asset; (4) a mean-variance formulation of portfolio selection; and (5) an equal rate for borrowing and lending and no capital rationing. Each author also assumes a perfect market.[5]

Among the questions that these authors investigate are the following: (1) What is the equilibrium relationship between portfolio risk (as measured by variance or standard deviation) and portfolio return? (2) What is the appropriate measure of risk for individual securities implied by the portfolio selection in the context of market equilibrium? (3) What is the relation between the risk of an individual security and its return?

[4] Lintner [15, 16] in places assumes that individuals are not in complete agreement about security parameters, although most of his work uses this assumption.
[5] Lintner [15, 16] again considers, or at least comments on, the effect that some imperfections may have on the results.

The Sharpe and Lintner models are analyzed in considerable detail in Chapter 7 of this book; the Mossin model is treated in Chapter 8. In the following pages, only a very brief review of the current work will be given.

**2.2.1. The Sharpe Model.** Sharpe [27] makes the five basic simplifying assumptions discussed in the previous section. He first represents the individual's utility function as $U = f(W, S)$ when $W$ is expected future wealth and $S$ is its standard deviation. (Sharpe uses standard deviation and not variance as the variable in his utility function.)

Sharpe then assumes that wealth available for investment $V_0$ is somehow exogenously determined and changes variables to expected return $\rho$ and its standard deviation $\sigma$.[6] Thus Sharpe uses a utility function $U = g(\rho, \sigma)$ in his analysis.

The essence of the Sharpe treatment is (1) If there were no riskless asset, the investment opportunities available to an investor would be a convex curve in the $(\rho, \sigma)$ plane.[7] (2) The existence of a riskless asset, however, means that the efficient frontier faced by each investor is a straight line tangent to the investment opportunity locus and intersecting the $\rho$ axis at the riskless rate. Any point on this line is a linear combination of the riskless asset and the tangency portfolio (cf. Figure 2.1). (3) Since all investors are in complete agreement about security parameters all will have the *same* efficient frontier; therefore, they will all desire to hold the same portfolio of risky assets and will borrow or lend according to their preference for risk-bearing as reflected in their utility function $U = g(\rho, \sigma)$. (4) If markets are not cleared,[8] then prices must adjust so that securities not in the tangency portfolio will be held. (5) The result of adjustment is a constant rate of substitution between risk and return at market equilibrium. Sharpe then employs the existence of linearity to relate the return on an individual security to the other security parameters.

Fama [6] not only presents a reformulation of the Sharpe derivation, given in this volume at the start of Chapter 7,[9] but shows that when reformulated

---

[6] This assumption precludes the holding of wealth in the form of securities *if* security prices are allowed to change. When wealth is held in the form of securities, the amount which individuals can invest depends on the prices. This point is important when one considers price adjustments that occur when the market is out of equilibrium, since $V_0$ depends on prices. The relation between variables is given by $W = (1 + \rho)V_0$ and $S = V_0\sigma$, where $V_0$ is the initial endowment of wealth.

[7] Convexity arises from the assumption of diminishing returns to risk-bearing.

[8] By explicitly requiring that supply equal demand for every security, we have extended Sharpe's model of equilibrium for completeness. Sharpe's only explicit requirement was that "capital asset prices must, of course, continue to change until a set of prices is attained for which every asset enters at least one combination lying on the capital market line" [26, p. 435]. However, market clearing is necessary for market equilibrium; it is implicit in Sharpe's concept of equilibrium. Thus, it is required that prices adjust until markets are cleared.

[9] Cf. Equations 7.6, 7.7, and 7.8.

the Sharpe and Lintner models have the same result for the risk premium on any given security.[10]

**2.2.2. The Lintner Model.** Lintner [15, 16] makes the basic assumptions of a perfect market, complete agreement,[11] the existence of a riskless asset, and the use of a mean-variance formulation. He first presents a qualitative argument analogous to Sharpe's and then focuses on the maximization of the quantity $\theta$ defined to be[12]

$$\theta = \frac{r - r_n}{\sigma_r}$$

where $r$ is the return on the portfolio of risky assets, $r_n$ is the riskless rate, and $\sigma_r$ is the standard deviation of $r$.

The quantity $\theta$ depends only on the investment in risky assets; it is independent of the investment in the riskless asset. The asset choice procedure of Lintner thus involves the following steps: (1) By maximizing $\theta$, choose a portfolio of risky assets. (2) Determine the investment in the riskless asset that will maximize the investor's utility function. In step (1), only the relative investment in risky assets is specified.[13] In step (2), the level of investment is specified and the degree of riskiness of the portfolio is determined. The locus of possible risk-return combinations is a linear curve in the risk-return plane.

From the asset-selection model, Lintner finds an expression for the risk premium for an individual security. The Lintner expression is

$$r_j - r_n = \lambda \sum_i \sigma_{ij} h_i,$$

where $r_j$ is the return on the $j$th risky security, $r_n$ is the return on the riskless asset, $\sigma_{ij}$ is the covariance between the $i$th and $j$th security, $h_i$ is the relative investment in the $i$th risky security ($\sum_i h_i = 1$), and $\lambda$ is a parameter.

Lintner explicitly considers the problem of price determination. Assuming that all investors agree on security parameters, Lintner shows that

$$h_j = \frac{p_j X_j}{T},$$

[10] The issue of the equivalence of the Sharpe and Lintner formulation and extensions to Fama's clarification are presented in Chapter 7.

[11] Lintner relaxes this assumption in some places.

[12] In Appendix 1 Lintner [15] argues that, given the various assumptions he has made, the maximization of $\theta$ is equivalent to maximization of a general utility function depending only on return and variance. See Chapter 7, especially Footnote 31 for further comment on the generality of maximizing $\theta$.

[13] Note that Lintner avoids having to generate the efficient frontier for risky assets by maximizing $\theta$.

where $p_j$ is the price of security $j$, $X_j$ is the total outstanding stock of security $j$, and $T$ is the total market value of all risky assets.[14]

### 2.2.3. The Mossin Model.

Mossin [19] presents a reasonably rigorous, lucid mean-variance model of market equilibrium that employs the conceptual framework of individuals choosing portfolios of assets in a perfect market. Mossin makes the simplifying assumptions of complete agreement among investors, a riskless asset, and unlimited borrowing. The Mossin formulation has some conceptual changes from the Sharpe–Lintner approach, including (1) the use of expected wealth and its variance as arguments of the utility function rather than expected return and its standard deviation; (2) the use of number of shares purchased as decision variables rather than relative wealth; (3) the endowment of each individual with an initial portfolio of securities rather than the assumption of an exogenously specified amount of wealth available for investment; and (4) the direct optimization of a mean-variance utility function subject to an explicit wealth constraint.

Mossin's mathematical formulation is the following: Let $\overline{U}(\overline{W}, V)$ be the expected utility of wealth where $\overline{W}$ is expected wealth and $V$ is its variance. Taking explicit cognizance of the wealth constraint, Mossin maximizes the Lagrangian

$$L = \overline{U}(\overline{W}, V) - \lambda \left[ \sum_{j=1}^{n} p_j(x_j - \hat{x}_j) \right],$$

where $p_j$ is price, $x_j$ is number of shares, and $\hat{x}_j$ is initial endowment of security $j$. Using the first-order conditions, Mossin obtains expressions for the rate of substitution of risk (variance) for wealth. Then he obtains a variety of equations for risk premiums. In considering the composition of equilibrium portfolios, Mossin [19, pp. 775 and 776] shows that "each individual will hold the same percentage of the total outstanding stock of each risky asset," which means that "the ratio between the holdings of the two risky assets is the same for all individuals" and that, at market equilibrium, each individual has a positive position in every security. These results depend on the assumption that all investors are in complete agreement about security parameters. Mossin also considers the market relation between return and risk and interprets the slope of this line as a measure of "the price of risk." Chapter 8 is devoted to an analysis and extension of the Mossin formulation of the mean-variance market equilibrium model.

[14] Although the Lintner equation is correct, it is not a valid method for determining prices because the set of equations is not independent (cf. Section 7.4.3. and especially Footnote 28).

# 3
# The
# Theory of
# Risk

The purpose of this chapter is to introduce a new general measure of risk, to investigate its properties, and to relate it to existing measures of risk. This new measure of risk will make possible the representation of expected utility in terms of two parameters, expected future wealth and risk, without imposing restrictions on either the form of the utility function or the nature of the probability distribution. With such a general risk-return representation of expected utility, we will be in a position to formulate a general single-period theory of asset selection.

## 3.1. The Generalized Risk Measure

It is assumed that individuals have a von Neumann–Morgenstern cardinal utility function and that a probability distribution for future wealth exists.

DEFINITION 3.1. A risk $\tilde{W}$ is the incurrence of the outcome of an event, the value of which is determined by a draw from a probability distribution.

An investor buying a portfolio of assets whose future value is a random variable $\tilde{W}$ is buying a risk. A gambler playing at a game of chance is also buying a risk. The distinction is primarily one of odds and complexity.

DEFINITION 3.2. The Generalized Risk Measure (GRM) is the difference in the utility of expected future wealth and the expected utility of future wealth, i.e.,

$$\phi = U(\overline{W}) - E[U(\tilde{W})] \tag{3.1}$$

where

$\phi$ = the Generalized Risk Measure
$\overline{W}$ = expected future wealth
$U$ = the utility function
$E$ = the expectation operator

The GRM $\phi$ will exist if $\overline{W}$, $U(\overline{W})$, and $E[U(\tilde{W})]$ exist; $\phi$ depends on both the form of utility function, the probability distribution for expected future wealth, and the mean of the distribution. Unlike variance, $\phi$ is not generally a property of only the probability distribution for wealth, but depends on the functional form of the utility function. $\phi$ is a global measure of risk. It will generally depend on $\overline{W}$ as well as properties of the probability distribution.

DEFINITION 3.3. An investor will be said to be *risk averse* if $\phi > 0$, *risk neutral* if $\phi = 0$, and *risk loving* if $\phi < 0$.

According to this definition, an investor will be risk averse if the utility of the mean of the distribution is greater than the expected utility of the distribution. This definition has the intuitive appeal of defining an investor to be risk averse if and only if he prefers the mean of the distribution for certain to taking a chance on a draw from the probability distribution. (It will be proved subsequently that these definitions of risk averseness are consistent with comparable definitions based on the risk premium.)

THEOREM 3.1. The following are true:
1. $\phi > 0$ if $U(W)$ is strictly concave
2. $\phi = 0$ if $U(W)$ is linear
3. $\phi < 0$ if $U(W)$ is strictly convex

PROOF.
1. Assume $U(W)$ is strictly concave. Then $U^{(2)}(W) < 0$ for all $W$. Expand $U(W)$ in Taylor's series about $\overline{W}$. Instead of an infinite expansion, use a three-term expansion, i.e.,

$$U(W) = U(\overline{W}) + U^{(1)}(\overline{W})(W - \overline{W}) + \tfrac{1}{2}U^{(2)}(\alpha\overline{W} + (1 - \alpha)W)(W - \overline{W})^2 \quad (3.2)$$

where $\alpha$ is a constant such that $0 \leq \alpha \leq 1$ and $U^{(1)}(\overline{W})$ and $U^{(2)}(\overline{W})$ are the first and second derivatives of $U(W)$ evaluated at $\overline{W}$. Then

$$E[U(\tilde{W})] = U(\overline{W}) + E[U^{(2)}(\alpha\overline{W} + (1 - \alpha)W)(W - \overline{W})^2] \quad (3.3)$$

$$\Rightarrow \phi = -E[(W - \overline{W})^2 U^{(2)}(\alpha\overline{W} + (1 - \alpha)W)]. \quad (3.4)$$

Since $U(W)$ is strictly concave everywhere,

$$U^{(2)}(\alpha\overline{W} + (1 - \alpha)W) < 0$$

for all values of $W$ regardless of the choice of $\alpha$. Since $(W - \overline{W})^2 > 0$, it follows that $\phi > 0$ regardless of the form of the probability density function.
2. For $U(W)$ convex, the proof is exactly the same as for when $U(W)$ is concave except the sign of $U^{(2)}(W)$ is reversed, and therefore $\phi < 0$.
3. Assume that $U(W)$ is linear. Let $U(W) = aW + b$ where $a > 0$. Then, $\overline{U} = a\overline{W} + b \Rightarrow \phi = U(\overline{W}) - \overline{U} = (a\overline{W} + b) - (a\overline{W} + b) = 0$.

Q.E.D.

The requirement that $U(W)$ be strictly concave or strictly convex can be relaxed. What is required for the proof is that $U(W)$ be concave (or convex) and be strictly concave (or strictly convex) over some interval where the probability on $W$ is not zero.

While it is true that a concave utility function will always be risk averse, concavity everywhere is not required for $\phi$ to be positive. For a particular risk, a curve of mixed concavity and convexity such as a Friedman–Savage utility function may produce $\phi > 0$ and therefore a risk-averse investor.[1]

### 3.2. Certainty Equivalents and the Risk Premium

DEFINITION 3.4. Given a risk $\tilde{W}$, the *certainty equivalent CE* is that amount such that the decision maker is exactly indifferent between receiving $CE$ for certain and taking a chance on the risk $\tilde{W}$.

DEFINITION 3.5. The risk premium $\pi$ for a risk $\tilde{W}$ is the difference between the expected value of the risk $\overline{W}$ and the certainty equivalent $CE$, i.e.,

$$\pi \equiv \overline{W} - CE. \tag{3.5}$$

This risk premium is measured in dollar units. It should not be confused with the difference in the return on a risky security and the return on a riskless security, which is measured in "interest rate" units, which is also called a *risk premium* in the literature, and which will be dicussed in Chapter 6, Section 6.2.1.

Thus, the risk premium $\pi$ is the amount by which the mean of the distribution must be changed such that an investor is indifferent between receiving $\overline{W} - \pi$ for certain and assuming the risk inherent in a draw from the probability distribution; therefore, by definition of $\pi$ it follows that

$$U(\overline{W} - \pi) = E[U(\tilde{W})]. \tag{3.6}$$

The risk premium will exist if $\overline{W}$, $U$, and $\overline{U}$ exist; $\pi$ depends on both the form of the utility function, the probability distribution, and the mean of the distribution.

The risk premium $\pi$ may be taken as a measure of the risk aversion of the decision-maker toward a given risk. The customary definition of risk averseness, risk neutrality, and risk loving are that $\pi$ be positive, zero, or negative, respectively.

As a measure of risk, $\pi$, like $\phi$, is a global measure. It is measured in dollar units while $\phi$ is measured in utility units. Both $\phi$ and $\pi$ will in general depend on (1) the form of the utility function; (2) the mean of the distribution; and (3) the form of the probability distribution for future wealth. The form of the utility function reflects attitudes toward risk-bearing; the form of the probability distribution reflects the properties of the risk being considered. The mean of the distribution determines the point on the utility function from which the risk will be viewed. If both the utility function and the mean of the probability distribution are fixed and *only* the shape of the probability distribution is allowed to vary about its fixed mean (say, by altering the dispersion), then the

[1] Cf. Friedman [8] for a discussion of utility functions that are concave in some regions and convex in others.

change in $\phi$ and the change in $\pi$ will be measures in the perceived change in riskiness.

The following theorem investigates the relation between $\phi$ and $\pi$ for a fixed utility function. It shows that $\phi$ and $\pi$ are closely related and that definitions of risk averseness, risk neutrality, or risk loving based on the signs of $\phi$ or $\pi$ are consistent if the utility function is strictly monotone increasing.

NOTATION. $(dx/dt)_z$ means the derivative of $x$ with respect to $t$ at constant $z$.

THEOREM 3.2. If $U(W)$ is strictly monotonic increasing and its functional form is fixed, then

1. $(d\phi/d\pi)_{\overline{W}} > 0$ for all $\overline{W}$ and the variables $\phi$ and $\pi$ are related by a one-to-one transformation.

2. The signs of $\phi$ and $\pi$ are equivalent as measures of risk aversion.

PROOF.

1. $\phi = U(\overline{W}) - \overline{U}$      by definition of $\phi$

     $= U(\overline{W}) - U(\overline{W} - \pi)$    by definition of $\pi$.

$\therefore \quad \left(\dfrac{d\phi}{d\pi}\right)_{\overline{W}} = U^{(1)}(\overline{W} - \pi) > 0$      if $U(W)$ is a monotone-increasing utility function.

2. $\phi\{\gtreqless\}0 \Leftrightarrow U(\overline{W}) - U(\overline{W} - \pi)\{\gtreqless\}0$

     $\Leftrightarrow \overline{W} - (\overline{W} - \pi)\{\gtreqless\}0$    since $U^{(1)} > 0$

     $\Leftrightarrow \pi\{\gtreqless\}0.$

                                                         Q.E.D.

Theorem 3.2. establishes that when $U(W)$ is a strictly monotone-increasing utility function, $\phi$ and $\pi$ are equivalent as measures of risk in the sense of being related by a one-to-one transformation. Hence, if a set of risks are ranked by the size of $\pi$, they would have the same ranking according to the size of $\phi$ for a given distribution mean $\overline{W}$. Theorem 3.2 also establishes that signs of $\phi$ and $\pi$ are equivalent as measures of risk averseness. For instance, one can speak of a decision-maker as being risk averse if $\phi > 0$ or if $\pi > 0$ and be completely consistent if $U(W)$ is a strictly monotone-increasing utility function.

Since utility functions that are not strictly monotone increasing are rather anomalous (if they exist at all), Theorem 3.2 establishes relations between $\phi$ and $\pi$ that are valid for essentially all "reasonable" utility functions.

Writing the generalized risk measure $\phi$ as

$$\phi = U(\overline{W}) - U(\overline{W} - \pi) = U(\overline{W}) - U(CE) \tag{3.7}$$

provides insight into the distinction between these two risk measures. $\pi$ is in

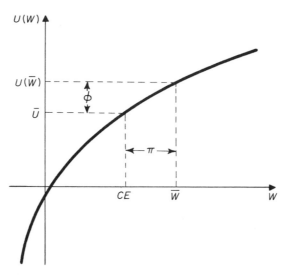

Fig. 3.1. The relation between $\phi$ and $\pi$.

monetary units (or in whatever units the numeraire is measured) and $\phi$ is in utility units. $\pi$ is the difference between the mean and the certainty equivalent, while $\phi$ is the difference between the utility of the mean and the utility of the certainty equivalent, $\overline{W} - \pi$. Thus, $\phi$ is a measure of the value of the risk premium—it indicates what the risk premium demanded by the individual means to the individuals in units in which value to the individual is measured.

In the unlikely event that $U(W)$ is not strictly monotone increasing, then the proof of Theorem 3.2 is not valid and the relations between $\phi$ and $\pi$ established therein may not hold. In fact, serious problems arise with $\pi$—it will not be uniquely defined and may be multivalued. If $U(W)$ is constant for some range of $W$, say from $W_1$ to $W_2$, and $\pi$ is such that $W_1 \leq \overline{W} - \pi \leq W_2$, then any other value of $\pi$ that keeps $\overline{W} - \pi$ in the range from $W_1$ to $W_2$ is a possible value of $\pi$; hence, $\pi$ is indeterminate. If $U(W)$ should actually decline, as, for example, occurs with a quadratic utility function, then $\pi$ is double-valued; see Figure 3.2 for a sketch indicating why $\pi$ is double-valued. In the figure, $\overline{U}$ and $\overline{W}$ are indicated as well as the two possible certainty equivalents, $W_1$ and $W_2$. The source of the problem is that there are two certainty equivalents, $W_1$ and $W_2$, such that $\overline{U} = U(W_1) = U(W_2)$, implying that there are two possible risk premiums, $\pi_1 = \overline{W} - W_1$ and $\pi_2 = \overline{W} - W_2$. Although $\pi_1$ seems to be the desired value since $\pi_2$ is negative, the resolution of the ambiguity is not always clear.

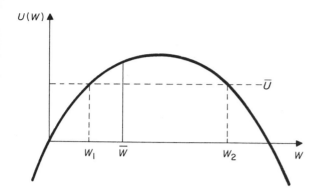

Fig. 3.2. A quadratic utility function.

For both of these pathological cases, $\phi$ remains well defined. Hence, $\phi$ is the more generally defined risk measure in the case of ill-defined utility functions.

THEOREM 3.3. If the utility function $U(W)$ is subject to the linear transformation $aU(W) + b$, then the GRM $\phi$ will be transformed by $a\phi$.

PROOF. Let $U^+(\overline{W}) = aU(W) + b$. Then the risk measure corresponding to $U^+(W)$ is

$$\phi^+ = U^+(\overline{W}) - \overline{U}^+$$
$$= a[U(\overline{W}) - \overline{U}]$$
$$\therefore \quad \phi^+ = a\phi.$$

Q.E.D.

Theorem 3.3 establishes that $\phi$ is invariant only to within a scale factor because a utility function is invariant only to within a linear transformation. Note that $\phi$ is not changed by a change in origin for $U(W)$ but only by the change in scale. The GRM $\phi$ is always measured in the units of utility.

Theorem 3.3 is independent of the distribution and its mean. The same transformation properties hold for any distribution and mean.

Unlike $\phi$, the risk premium $\pi$ is independent of the scale of the utility function since $c \cdot U(\overline{W} - \pi) = c\overline{U}$ if $U(\overline{W} - \pi) = \overline{U}$ for any constant $c$. Thus, $\pi$ is scale invariant for changes in the scale of the utility function. Of course, if one changes the units in which one measures wealth, for instance from dollars to pennies, then the scale for $\pi$ will change accordingly.

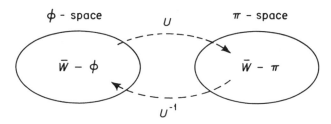

Fig. 3.3. $\phi$ —space and $\pi$ —space.

A particular choice of scale that is of some interest is the case for which $U(\overline{W}) = \overline{W}$. Assume $U(W)$ is such that $\pi$ is well defined. Then

$$\phi = \overline{W} - \overline{U} = \overline{W} - U(\overline{W} - \pi) \qquad \text{if} \quad U(\overline{W}) = \overline{W}$$

$$\Rightarrow U(\overline{W} - \pi) = \overline{W} - \phi \tag{3.8}$$

$$\Rightarrow U^{-1}(\overline{W} - \phi) = \overline{W} - \pi. \tag{3.9}$$

These last two equations have the following symmetry property: they are unchanged if $\phi$ and $\pi$ are interchanged and if $U$ and $U^{-1}$ are interchanged. When $U(\overline{W}) = \overline{W}$, both $\phi$ and $\pi$ measure the effect of risk bearing by reducing (or, more generally, by altering) the value of $\overline{W}$. One can think of a "$\phi$-space" and a "$\pi$-space" connected by the transformation $U$, as shown in Figure 3.3.

The fact that a particular choice of the scale and/or origin is necessary to make $U(\overline{W}) = \overline{W}$ means that the practical use of Equations 3.8 and 3.9 are limited. However, the symmetry property and the concept of $\phi$-space and $\pi$-space help to interpret $\phi$ and $\pi$.

To summarize:
1. A new risk measure $\phi = U(\overline{W}) - \overline{U}$ has been introduced.
2. The new risk measure $\phi$ is such that $\phi > 0$ if $U(W)$ is concave, $\phi = 0$ everywhere if $U(W)$ is linear, and $\phi < 0$ if $U(W)$ is convex.
3. The risk measure $\phi$ is related to the risk premium $\pi$ by a monotonic transformation; $(d\phi/d\pi)_{\overline{W}} > 0$ when $U(W)$ is strictly monotone increasing and $\overline{W}$ is fixed and only the shape of the probability distribution is allowed to change.
4. $\phi\{\gtreqless\}0$ if and only if $\pi\{\gtreqless\}0$ when $U(W)$ is strictly monotone increasing; the signs of $\phi$ and $\pi$ are thus equivalent indicators of risk aversion ($\phi > 0$, $\pi > 0$), risk neutrality ($\phi = 0$, $\pi = 0$), and risk loving ($\phi < 0$, $\pi < 0$).
5. When $U$ is not monotonic increasing, $\pi$ will be multivalued for some values of $\overline{W}$ and thus is not well defined; $\phi$ is still single-valued and well defined if $U(\overline{W})$ and $\overline{U}$ exist.

6. $\pi$ is invariant when the utility function is subject to a linear transformation; $\phi$ is invariant only to within a constant scale factor. However, once the units in which utility is measured are fixed, $\phi$ will not change.

To these six points we add the observation that in $\overline{U} = U(\overline{W}) - \phi$, $\phi$ is "outside" the utility function while in $\overline{U} = U(\overline{W} - \pi)$, $\pi$ is "inside" the utility function. This means that $\phi$ may be more accessible in studying risk-return relationships.

Both $\phi$ and $\pi$ are global measures of risk that reflect the interaction of the individual's utility function and subjective probability distribution. The issue of whether $\phi$ or $\pi$ best measures risk is unresolved; the question of whether $\phi$ or $\pi$ produces a simpler expression for risk will turn out to depend on the particular utility function and distribution being considered. Thus, the question of whether $\phi$ or $\pi$ is the better global measure of risk is not readily answerable in the absence of well-defined criteria for determining the superiority of risk measures. It is this author's opinion that both have merit, that both can provide insight into the characterization and study of decision-making under risk, and that both should be considered in theoretical studies of risk-return relationships.

The use of either $\phi$ or $\pi$ enables expected utility to be represented in terms of risk and return without making special assumptions about the form of either the utility function or of the probability distribution for future wealth. Thus, either risk measure will enable us to derive general properties of portfolio risk, security risk, and equilibrium risk-return relationships without placing severe and probably unrealistic restrictions on the form of the utility function.

### 3.3. A Series Expression for the General Risk Measure

For some utility functions and probability distributions it is possible to expand $U(W)$ in a Taylor series about $\overline{W}$ and obtain a useful expression for $\phi$ in terms of moments of the probability distribution and derivatives of the utility function.

THEOREM 3.4. If $U(W)$ is a cardinal utility function such that
1. the Taylor's expansion about $\overline{W}$ exists for $U(W)$ in a neighborhood about $\overline{W}$;
2. the neighborhood about $\overline{W}$ is sufficiently large to include all $W$ for which there is a nonzero probability of occurrence; and
3. the probability distribution for $\tilde{W}$ is such that all central moments exist,
Then, the risk measure $\phi$ is given by

$$\phi = -\sum_{k=2}^{\infty} \frac{U^{(k)}(\overline{W})M_k}{k!} \tag{3.10}$$

where $M_k$ is the $k$th central moment of the probability distribution and

$U^{(k)}(\overline{W})$ is the $k$th derivative of $U(W)$ evaluated at the mean of the distribution $\overline{W}$.

PROOF. Expand $U(W)$ in a Taylor's expansion about $\overline{W}$. Then,

$$U(W) = U(\overline{W}) + U^{(1)}(\overline{W})(W - \overline{W}) + \sum_{k=2}^{\infty} \frac{U^{(k)}(\overline{W})(W - \overline{W})^k}{k!} \tag{3.11}$$

$$\Rightarrow E[U(W)] = U(\overline{W}) + \sum_{k=2}^{\infty} \frac{U^{(k)}(\overline{W})M_k}{k!} \tag{3.12}$$

$$\Rightarrow \phi = U(\overline{W}) - E[U(W)] = -\sum_{k=2}^{\infty} \frac{U^{(k)}(\overline{W})M_k}{k!}. $$

Q.E.D.

Equation 3.10 displays the interaction of the utility function and the probability distribution in an interesting manner. It asserts that $\phi$ is the sum of the moments of the probability distribution weighted by the corresponding derivative of the utility function evaluated at $\overline{W}$. The fact that the $k$th derivative of $U(W)$ determines the importance of the $k$th central moment is surprising!

The requirement that the Taylor's expansion for $U(W)$ converge for all $W$ for which the probability of occurrence is nonzero is fairly stringent. Another weaker version of the theorem could be developed in terms of stochastic convergence. However, this generality is not required for the purposes of this book. A variant of the theorem that is useful involves Taylor's expansion with a remainder. In this case, it can be shown that $\phi$ is given by

$$\phi = -\sum_{k=2}^{n} \frac{U^{(k)}(\overline{W})M_k}{k!} + E[R_n(\tilde{W}; \overline{W})] \tag{3.13}$$

where $R_n(\overline{W}; W)$, the $n$th order remainder of the Taylor's expansion about $\overline{W}$, is given by

$$R_n(W; \overline{W}) = \frac{U^{(n+1)}(\alpha W + (1 - \alpha)\overline{W}) \cdot (W - \overline{W})^{n+1}}{(n + 1)!} \quad \text{for } 0 \leq \alpha \leq 1. \tag{3.14}$$

In subsequent sections of this chapter, some particular utility functions for which the Taylor's series exists will be introduced and Equation 3.10 evaluated.

### 3.4. Risk Aversion in the Small

In his paper "Risk Aversion in the Small and in the Large," John W. Pratt [22] defined and analyzed a measure of local risk aversion.

DEFINITION 3.6. The Pratt measure of local risk aversion $r(\overline{W})$ is defined as

$$r(\overline{W}) = -\frac{U^{(2)}(\overline{W})}{U^{(1)}(\overline{W})} \tag{3.15}$$

where $U(\overline{W})$ is the utility function for wealth and $U^{(1)}(\overline{W})$ and $U^{(2)}(\overline{W})$ are first-order and second-order derivatives.

Pratt developed $r(W)$ by expanding $U(W - \pi)$ and $\overline{U}$ for a small risk (one with small variance) and letting variance go to zero. To first order the risk premium $\pi$ is then given by

$$\pi = \tfrac{1}{2} r(\overline{W}) s^2 \tag{3.16}$$

where $s$ is the standard deviation of $W$.

This risk measure is local in the sense that it is a point measure that considers the value of derivatives of $U(W)$ at the point $\overline{W}$.

We shall not in this book consider the Pratt article in depth, but will restrict our attention to investigating the relation of the GRM $\phi$ to the local measure of risk aversion, $r(W)$.

In Equation 3.10, $\phi$ is given by

$$\phi = -\sum_{k=2}^{\infty} \frac{U^{(k)}(\overline{W}) M_k}{k!}.$$

Dropping all terms but the first, it is seen that

$$\phi \doteq \frac{U^{(2)}(\overline{W}) s^2}{2} \tag{3.17}$$

$$\therefore \quad \phi = +\frac{U^{(1)}(\overline{W}) r(\overline{W}) s^2}{2}. \tag{3.18}$$

Recognizing $r(\overline{W}) s^2 / 2$ as the approximation for the risk premium derived by Pratt, Equation 3.18 asserts that for small risks $\phi$ is the marginal utility of wealth times the risk premium to the order of accuracy involved in the approximations, i.e.,

$$\phi \doteq \frac{dU(\overline{W})}{dW} \cdot \pi = (\text{marginal utility}) \cdot (\text{risk premium}). \tag{3.19}$$

This expression is consistent with the result that $\phi$ is the utility measure of what the risk premium means to the individual.

## 3.5. Some Examples of the GRM $\phi$

In the following sections specific utility functions will be assumed and the generalized risk measure will be investigated. Included in the utility functions to be investigated are the quadratic, exponential, and logarithmic. Closed-form utility functions are used to provide computational ease. Among the issues to be investigated are equations relating $\phi$ and $\pi$, a series expression for $\phi$, and approximations for $\phi$.

**3.5.1. The Quadratic Utility Function.** In this section we shall obtain expressions for $\phi$ and $\pi$ in terms of parameters of a quadratic utility function and the distribution function and then relate $\phi$ and $\pi$.

Let $U(W) = aW - bW^2$ where $b > 0$. Then, assuming that the second moment exists, expected utility and the generalized risk measure are given by

$$\overline{U} = a\overline{W} - bE[W^2] \tag{3.20}$$

$$\phi = U(\overline{W}) - \overline{U} = -b(\overline{W}^2 - E[W^2]) = bV(W), \tag{3.21}$$

where $V(W)$ is the variance of $W$.

Thus, if $U(W)$ is a quadratic utility function, the generalized risk measure $\phi$ is proportional to variance for every distribution for which variance exists. This result is consistent with the widespread use of variance as a risk measure for quadratic utility functions.

One can derive an expression for the risk premium by equating $\overline{U}$ and $U(\overline{W} - \pi)$. Equating $\overline{U}$ as given by Equation 3.20 and $U(\overline{W} - \pi)$ and solving for $\pi$ gives

$$\pi = -\frac{(a - 2b\overline{W}) \pm \sqrt{(a - 2b\overline{W})^2 + 4b^2 V(W)}}{2b}. \tag{3.22}$$

This equation for $\pi$ is considerably more complex than the expression for $\phi$ given by Equation 3.21. The fact that $\pi$ is double-valued arises from the fact that $U(W) = aW - bW^2$ is not strictly monotonic. The quadratic utility is a specific example of the problem with $\pi$ when $U$ is not a monotone increasing utility function.

The relation between $\phi$ and $\pi$ is obtained by equating $U(\overline{W}) - \phi$ and $U(\overline{W} - \pi)$. For the case of a quadratic utility function, one obtains

$$\phi = (a - 2b\overline{W})\pi + b\pi^2. \tag{3.23}$$

To summarize, for a quadratic utility, the generalized risk measure $\phi$ is proportional to the variance and is a quadratic function of the risk premium $\pi$; the risk premium $\pi$ is a function of the mean, the variance, and the parameters of the utility function and is double-valued.

**3.5.2. The Exponential Utility Function.** The utility function $U(W) = 1 - e^{-cW}$ and $U(W) = -e^{-cW}$ are equivalent, common expressions for the exponential utility function. We shall use $U(W) = -e^{-cW}$ in the following analysis.

Before proceeding with the analysis, we remark that the exponential utility function has been shown by Pratt [22] to possess constant (local) risk aversion in the sense of the risk measure $r(\overline{W}) \equiv -[U^{(2)}(\overline{W})/U^{(1)}(\overline{W})]$. In this case, $r(\overline{W}) = +c$.

To obtain the relation between $\phi$ and $\pi$, we equate $U(\overline{W}) - \phi$ and $U(\overline{W} - \pi)$ and solve as follows:

$$-e^{-c\overline{W}} - \phi = -e^{-c(\overline{W} - \pi)}$$

$$\Rightarrow \phi = e^{-c\overline{W}}(e^{c\pi} - 1). \tag{3.24}$$

Since $U(W) = -e^{-cW}$ is strictly concave, both $\phi$ and $\pi$ are positive. A sketch of $\phi$ vs $\pi$ is given in Figure 3.4.

We shall now obtain an expression for $\phi$ by using the equation for $\phi$ based on the Taylor's expansion given by Equation 3.10. The $k$th-order derivative of $U(W)$ is given by

$$U^{(k)}(W) = (-1)^{k+1}c^k e^{-cW}. \tag{3.25}$$

Substituting this expression into Equation 3.10 gives

$$\phi = e^{-c\overline{W}} \sum_{k=2}^{\infty} \frac{(-1)^k c^k M_k}{k!}, \tag{3.26}$$

where it is assumed that $M_k$ exists. (Convergence is guaranteed by the fact that the Taylor series expansion for $e^{-cW}$ converges for all finite $W$.) Note that $\phi$ depends on the distribution mean $\overline{W}$, the scale parameter $c$, and on all central moments. From Equations 3.24 and 3.26, we obtain

$$e^{c\pi} - 1 = \sum_{k=2}^{\infty} \frac{(-1)^k c^k M_k}{k!} \tag{3.27}$$

$$\Rightarrow \pi = \frac{\log\left[1 + \dfrac{\sum_{k=2}^{\infty} (-1)^k c^k M_k}{k!}\right]}{c} \tag{3.28}$$

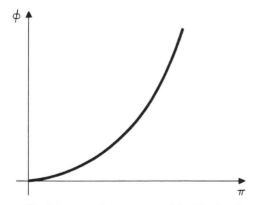

Fig. 3.4. $\phi$ vs. $\pi$ for an exponential utility function.

To obtain an approximation for $\phi$, take the first four terms of the series given by Equation 3.26. Then

$$\phi \doteq e^{-c\overline{W}} \left( \frac{c^2 M_2}{2} - \frac{c^3 M_3}{3!} + \frac{c^4 M_4}{4!} - \frac{c^5 M_5}{5!} + - \cdots \right). \tag{3.29}$$

If the distribution for $W$ is symmetric about the mean, then the odd central moments vanish and $\phi$ is given by

$$\phi \doteq e^{-c\overline{W}} \left( \frac{c^2 M_2}{2} + \frac{c^4 M_4}{24} + \cdots \right). \tag{3.30}$$

If the distribution is skewed, then we see that left-skewness increases the risk function, since $M_3 < 0$ for left-skewness; and right-skewness decreases the risk function, since $M_3 > 0$ for right-skewness. Thus, the common intuitive feeling that right-skewness is desirable and left-skewness is highly undesirable to a risk-averse portfolio selector is quantitatively reflected in the risk measure $\phi$. A two-term approximation for $\phi$ that reflects the effect of the first two moments is

$$\phi \doteq e^{-c\overline{W}} \left( \frac{c^2 M_2}{2} - \frac{c^3 M_3}{6} \right). \tag{3.31}$$

The validity of this approximation (or of a four-term expression that could also be obtained from Equation 3.29) depends on the magnitude of $c$ and of the moments. Clearly, a value of $c < 1$ will enhance convergence and the validity of the approximation.

**3.5.3. Other Utility Functions.** The reader may analyze other utility functions in a manner analogous to the work of the preceding section. Table 3.1 summarizes such an analysis for some possible utility functions, including $\log W$, $-W^{-1}$, and $\sqrt{W}$ in addition to those already analyzed.

Observe that right-skewness reduces the risk measure $\phi$ in all of the examples. Also note that $\phi = 0$ wherever $\pi = 0$. Some of the utility functions are not defined for all $W$, e.g. $\log W$ is defined only for $W > 0$ and $-W^{-1}$ is meaningfully defined as a utility function only for $W > 0$. Consequently, the series expression for $\phi$ in terms of moments of the probability distribution is valid only for distributions that have no probability of having $W$ be less than zero. The log-normal distribution is one candidate that does preclude negative $W$ and that has some empirical validity for describing portfolio distributions.

**3.5.4. The Normal Distribution—An Example.** If $W$ is distributed according to a normal distribution, then expected utility can be represented as a function of the distribution mean and variance, i.e.,

$$E[U(W)] = g(\overline{W}, V) \tag{3.32}$$

TABLE 3.1. THE GRM $\phi$ FOR VARIOUS UTILITY FUNCTIONS.

| Utility Fn | $\phi(\pi)$ | $\phi$ | 2-Term Approximation |
|---|---|---|---|
| 1. $a + bW$ | $\phi = \pi = 0$ | $\phi = 0$ | n.a. |
| 2. $aW - bW^2$ | $\phi = (a - 2b\overline{W})\pi + b\pi^2$ | $\phi = bM_2$ | n.a. |
| 3. $-e^{-W}$ | $\phi = -[e^{-\overline{W}} - e^{-(\overline{W} - \pi)}]$ | $\phi = e^{-\overline{W}} \displaystyle\sum_{k=2}^{\infty} \frac{(-1)^{k+1} M_k}{k!}$ | $e^{-\overline{W}}\left(\dfrac{M_2}{2} - \dfrac{M_3}{6}\right)$ |
| 4. $\log W$ | $\phi = -\log\left(1 - \dfrac{\pi}{\overline{W}}\right)$ | $\phi = \displaystyle\sum_{k=2}^{\infty} \frac{(-1)^k M_k}{\overline{W}^k k!}$ | $\dfrac{M_2}{2\overline{W}^2} - \dfrac{M_3}{3\overline{W}^3}$ |
| 5. $-\dfrac{1}{W}$ | $\phi = \dfrac{\pi}{\overline{W}(\overline{W} - \pi)}$ | $\phi = \displaystyle\sum_{k=2}^{\infty} \frac{(-1)^k M_k}{\overline{W}^{k+1}}$ | $\dfrac{M_2}{\overline{W}^3} - \dfrac{M_3}{\overline{W}^4}$ |
| 6. $\sqrt{W}$ | $\phi = 1 - \sqrt{1 - \dfrac{\pi}{\overline{W}}}$ | $\phi = \displaystyle\sum_{k=2}^{\infty} \frac{(-1)^k (2k - 2)! \overline{W}^{-[(2k-1)/2]} M_k}{k! \cdot (k - 1)! 2k}$ | $\dfrac{\overline{W}^{-(3/2)} M_2}{6} - \dfrac{\overline{W}^{-(5/2)} M_3}{16}$ |

for some function $g$, where $V$ is variance. This fact has frequently been used to justify variance as the measure of portfolio risk.

The fact that expected utility can be represented in terms of mean and variance really means that risk can be represented as a function of mean and variance and possibly a function of variance alone. In the following, $\phi$ is derived for the exponential utility function under a normal distribution.

For the case of a normal distribution, the Taylor series expression for $\phi$ given by Equation 3.10 can be specialized. For a normal distribution, the odd moments are zero and the even moments are given by[2]

$$M_k = (k - 1)!! \, s^k \tag{3.33}$$

where $s$ is the standard deviation, and

$$(k - 1)!! \equiv (k - 1)(k - 3)(k - 5)\ldots 5 \cdot 3 \cdot 1. \tag{3.34}$$

Using the fact that odd moments are zero in Equation 3.10 gives

$$\phi = -\sum_{k=1}^{\infty} \frac{U^{(2k)}(\overline{W})M_{2k}}{(2k)!} \tag{3.35}$$

Substituting the expression for $M_k$ given by Equation (3.33) and simplifying gives

$$\therefore \quad \phi = -\sum_{k=1}^{\infty} \frac{U^{(2k)}(\overline{W})s^{2k}}{2^k k!} \tag{3.36}$$

Recall that the Taylor's series expansion for the utility function $U(W)$ must converge for all finite $W$ for the expression above to hold since the range of the normal distribution is from $-\infty$ to $+\infty$.

To illustrate the use of Equation 3.36, consider again the exponential utility function $U(W) = -e^{-cW}$. The even derivatives are given by

$$U^{(2k)}(\overline{W}) = -c^{2k}e^{-c\overline{W}} \qquad k = 1, 2, 3, 4, \ldots$$

$$\therefore \quad \phi = e^{-c\overline{W}} \sum_{k=1}^{\infty} \frac{c^{2k}s^{2k}}{2^k k!} = e^{-c\overline{W}} \sum_{k=1}^{\infty} \frac{1}{k!}\left(\frac{c^2 s^2}{2}\right)^k$$

$$\Rightarrow \phi = e^{-c\overline{W}}(e^{c^2 s^2/2} - 1) \quad \text{since} \sum_{n=1}^{\infty} \frac{x^n}{n!} = e^x - 1 \tag{3.37}$$

From Equation 3.24 it is clear that $\pi$ is given by

$$\pi = cs^2/2. \tag{3.38}$$

Equation 3.37 asserts that $\phi$ increases exponentially with variance. Note that

[2] See Appendix 2 for a derivation of this expression.

$\phi = 0$ when $s = 0$. Note also that $\phi$ does depend on $\overline{W}$, the mean of the distribution.

What is particularly interesting is that the expression for $\pi$ given by Equation 3.38 is the same as the expression for $\pi$ given by the Pratt approximation, since $r(W) = -U^{(2)}(\overline{W})/U^{(1)}(\overline{W}) = +c$ and, from Equation 3.16, $\pi$ is given by $\pi = 1/2r(\overline{W})s^2 = cs^2/2$.

## 3.6. Two-Parameter Utility Functions

The purpose of introducing the risk measure $\phi$ was to make possible the expression of expected utility in terms of expected future wealth $\overline{W}$ and risk $\phi$ without imposing serious restrictions on the form of either the utility function or the distribution function. In the process of analyzing $\phi$, it became clear that in many cases the existing mean-variance models did not conform to the structure of the risk measure $\phi$, as was expected, since mean-variance models require fairly severe restrictions (e.g., normality) to be rigorously valid.

In order to develop a general model of asset selection and asset pricing that will include both the work on risk developed in this chapter and the mean-variance models of Sharpe, Lintner, and Mossin, we shall postulate a very general representation of expected utility. The definition of such a representation is given below along with the formal definition of a representation of expected utility based on the risk measure $\phi$.

### 3.6.1. The TPFR and the GMC

DEFINITION 3.7. *The Two-Parameter Functional Representation* (TPFR) is an expression for expected utility of the form

$$E[U(\tilde{W})] = f(\overline{W}, \psi) \qquad (3.39)$$

where $E[U(\tilde{W})]$ is expected utility, $f$ is some function, $\overline{W}$ is the mean of the distribution, and $\psi$ is some measure of risk.

DEFINITION 3.8. *The Generalized Markowitz Criterion* (GMC) is a representation of expected utility in the form

$$E[U(\tilde{W})] = U(\overline{W}) - \phi \qquad (3.40)$$

where $E[U(\tilde{W})]$ is expected utility, $\overline{W}$ is the mean of the distribution, and $\phi$ is the general risk measure.

The GMC arises from the definition of the risk measure $\phi$ and is consequently a valid risk-return representation if one accepts $\phi$ as a valid measure. The TPFR is simply the postulation of the representation of expected utility as *some* function of the return and *some* measure of risk $\psi$. For a given risk measure $\psi$, there is no guarantee that the TPFR will exist or have any given set of requisite properties. The reason for introducing the TPFR is not descriptive accuracy but generality—it should be possible to represent any two-parameter representation of expected utility in the form of the TPFR including the GMC and the mean-variance models of Sharpe, Lintner, and Mossin. The TPFR will be used for this purpose in Chapter 5. For any particular specification of $\psi$ and $U(W)$, one must determine the particular form of the function $f$ for the TPFR.

The GMC is clearly a special case of the TPFR in which $\psi \equiv \phi$ and $f(\overline{W}, \psi) \equiv U(\overline{W}) - \psi$.

The representation of expected utility in terms of the risk premium $\pi$, $U(\overline{W} - \pi)$, is also another special case of the TPFR in which $\psi \equiv \pi$ and $f(\overline{W}, \psi) \equiv U(\overline{W} - \psi)$.

**3.6.2. The TPFR and M-V Models.** The TPFR includes the existing mean-variance models of Sharpe, Lintner, and Mossin as special cases. To obtain the Sharpe or Lintner models, let $\psi = s$, the standard deviation of wealth. Then $\overline{U} = f(\overline{W}, s)$ for some unspecified function $f$. Both Sharpe and Lintner treated portfolio return and its standard deviation as variables. To get this representation, let $\rho$ and $\sigma$ be portfolio return and its standard deviation and let $V_0$ be the initial endowment of wealth. Then

$$\overline{W} = (1 + \bar{\rho})V_0$$

$$s = \sigma V_0.$$

Then, $f(\overline{W}, s)$ becomes $f[(1 + \bar{\rho})V_0, \sigma V_0] \equiv F(\bar{\rho}, \sigma)$ where $F$ is a new function. To get the specific form of $F(\bar{\rho}, \sigma)$ used by Lintner in much of his work, write

$$F(\bar{\rho}, \sigma) = \frac{\bar{\rho} - r_n}{\sigma}$$

where $r_n$ is the expected return on the riskless asset.

To obtain the Mossin objective function, let $\psi = V$, where $V$ is variance of wealth. Then, $f(\overline{W}, \psi) = f(\overline{W}, V)$. Mossin did not specify $f$ any further, but used a general functional representation of the mean-variance model.

**3.6.3. The Critical Nature of the Issue of the Risk Measure.** If one is to investigate issues such as the measure of security risk implied by equilibrium or the relation between risk and return at market equilibrium, one must be careful about specifying correctly both the measure of portfolio risk and the functional dependence of expected utility on this measure of portfolio risk, since the implied measure of security risk and the equilibrium risk-return relationship will clearly depend on these specifications.

The problems of M-V models are that their applicability is very limited and that there is no clear rationale for specifying whether the risk measure should be standard deviation, variance, or even possibly some linear combination of the two. These problems will be discussed in more detail in subsequent chapters.

**4**
**The Basic**
**Equilibrium**
**Model**

The purpose of this chapter is to set forth the basic model that will be developed and analyzed in subsequent chapters. We first define terms and introduce the conventions and notation that will be used throughout the rest of the book. We then present formally the basic assumptions, discuss them, and indicate what assumptions have not been made. Then the equilibrium model is analyzed without making use of either of the two-parameter objective functions developed in the previous chapter. The reason for this general analysis is to show clearly what result can be obtained without the use of two-parameter objective functions and to relate this work to the standard treatment of general equilibrium. Finally, a note on the incorporation of the consumption decision into the investment-selection model is presented.

### 4.1. Conventions and Notation

Before proceeding with the development of the model, basic terms will be discussed and the conventions and notation will be summarized.

**4.1.1. Basic Terms.** A *security* will mean any asset that is bought or sold in the market under consideration. *Individual* will mean any entity that buys and sells assets; the term *individual* and *investor* will be used interchangeably. A *share* is the unit of an asset for which a price is quoted. *Position in a security* will mean the number of shares held of that security. An individual's *portfolio position* or *position vector* will be the number of shares of each security held by the individual.

**4.1.2. Conventions.** A *superscript* on a variable will denote an individual unless it is enclosed in parentheses; then it will denote a derivative. For instance, $\phi^i$ is the risk function of individual $i$.

A *subscript* will usually denote a security. (Exceptions to this rule will be obvious from the context of their uses.)

Vectors will be printed in **boldface** type, matrixes in sans serif type for Latin letters and lightface for Greek letters. A prime on a vector or matrix will indicate the transpose. Vectors, unless explicitly defined otherwise, will be column vectors. A tilde over a symbol will denote a random variable; a bar over the symbol will denote mean value.

When a derivative is taken with some variable held constant, this fact will be denoted by subscripting the derivative with the variable. For instance, $[(\partial W^i)/(\partial x_j^i)]_{\mathbf{p}}$ means the vector of prices $\mathbf{p}$ is held constant. The subscript $n$ will be used for the riskless asset when it exists.

A caret over a symbol will denote "the initial value" of a variable, e.g., $\hat{x}_j^i$ is the initial value of individual $i$'s holding of security $j$.

### 4.1.3. Notation

$m$ = number of individuals.

$n$ = number of securities.

$x_j^i$ = number of shares of security $j$ held by individual $i$.

$\mathbf{x}^i = (x_1^i, x_2^i, \ldots, x_n^i)$ is an $n$-dimensional portfolio vector for individual $i$.

$\hat{x}_j^i$ = initial endowment of individual $i$ with shares of security $j$.

$\hat{\mathbf{x}}^i$ = initial portfolio vector for individual $i$.

$y_j^i$ = fraction of individual $i$'s wealth invested in security $j$.

$h_j^i$ = fraction of the wealth invested in risky securities by individual $i$ in security $j$. (Note that $h_j^i$ is meaningful only when there exists a riskless asset.)

$\mathbf{y} = (y_1, y_2, \ldots, y_n)$ = vector of relative amount invested in all securities.

$\mathbf{h} = (h_1, h_2, \ldots, h_{n-1})$ = vector of relative amount invested in the first $n-1$ securities.

$\mu_j^i$ = price expected by individual $i$ for one share of security $j$ at the end of the time period. (Note that $\mu_j^i$ is the expected price; the random variable will be denoted by $\tilde{\mu}_j^i$.)

$p_j$ = current price of security $j$.

$r_j^i = \dfrac{\mu_j^i}{p_j} - 1$ = return expected by individual $i$ on security $j$.

$m_j^i = r_j^i - r_n^i$ = risk premium on security $j$ when asset $n$ is riskless.

$\mathbf{m} = (m_1, m_2, \ldots, m_{n-1})$ = vector of risk premiums. (This vector $\mathbf{m}$ should not be confused with the number of individuals $m$; the symbol $m$ will refer to a risk premium only if it has a subscript or if it is a vector. Otherwise, $m$ = number of individuals.)

$\mathbf{r} = (r_1, \ldots, r_{n-1})$ = vector of returns on the first $n-1$ assets.

$r^i = \displaystyle\sum_{j=1}^{n-1} r_j h_j$ = expected return on the first $n-1$ risky securities.

$\rho^i = \displaystyle\sum_{j=1}^{n} r_j y_j$ = expected return on the portfolio.

$\overline{W}^i = \displaystyle\sum_{j=1}^{n} \mu_j^i x_j^i$ = expected wealth of individual $i$ one period away.

$V_0^i = \displaystyle\sum_{j=1}^{n} p_j \hat{x}_j^i$ = current value of individual $i$'s endowment when he enters the market.

$\phi^i = \phi^i(x_1^i, \ldots, x_n^i)$ = a general risk function for individual $i$ with portfolio $\mathbf{x}^i = (x_1^i, \ldots, x_n^i)$ to be used in the GMC.

$\psi^i = \psi^i(x_1^i, \ldots, x_n^i)$ = a general measure of risk for individual $i$ with portfolio $\mathbf{x}^i = (x_1^i, \ldots, x_n^i)$ to be used in the TPFR.

$$\Phi^i = \frac{\phi^i}{V_0^i} = \text{risk per dollar in the GMC.}$$

$$\Psi^i = \frac{\psi^i}{V^i} = \text{risk per dollar in the TPFR.}$$

$$\Psi_j^i = \frac{1}{p_j}\left(\frac{\partial\psi^i}{\partial x_j^i}\right)_{\mathbf{p}} = \text{marginal risk per dollar at constant prices in the TPFR.}$$

$$\Phi_j^i = \frac{1}{p_j}\left(\frac{\partial\phi^i}{\partial x_j^i}\right)_{\mathbf{p}} = \text{marginal risk per dollar at constant prices in the GMC.}$$

### 4.2. Basic Assumptions

The following are the basic assumptions of the model.

A1. All investors have the same single-period time horizon.

A2. Investors enter the market with expectations about the future performance of individual securities. These expectations can be represented as distributions on the *future* price of each security at the end of the time period. (*Future price* includes any dividends that a security will pay between now and the end of the time period; taxes are ignored in the sense that no distinction is made between dividends and capital gains.)

A3. Each investor maximizes the expected utility of his end-of-the-period *wealth*. Different investors will generally have different utility functions and different probability distributions for the performance of individual securities and, therefore, for the probability distribution of expected future wealth.

A4. Expected utility can be represented as a function of two parameters, return and risk. Two different two-parameter representations will be used. These are the two-parameter functional representation (TPFR) and the generalized Markowitz criterion (GMC). Using superscripts to denote individual $i$, these are, respectively,

$$E^i[U^i(\tilde{W}^i)] = f^i(\overline{W}^i, \psi^i)$$

$$E^i[U^i(\tilde{W}^i)] = U^i(\overline{W}^i) - \phi^i.$$

A5. The $x_j^i$'s are completely divisible. (Fractional shares may be held.) The risk function of an individual is a continuous, differentiable function of the $x_j^i$'s.

A6. Short sales are permitted, and therefore the allowable range of values of $x_j^i$ is unrestricted.

A7. Investors enter the market with an initial endowment of securities. This endowment is given by

$$\hat{x}^i = (\hat{x}_1^i, \hat{x}_2^i, \dots, \hat{x}_n^i) \qquad i = 1, \dots, m.$$

A8. Investors are subject to a wealth constraint given by

$$\sum_{j=1}^{n} p_j x_j^i = \sum_{j=1}^{n} p_j \hat{x}_j^i.$$

A9. The number of outstanding shares of a security is constant, i.e.,

$$\sum_{i=1}^{n} x_j^i \equiv X_j \qquad j = 1, \ldots, n.$$

Thus, the issue of new shares during the analysis is not permitted.

A10. The price of any security is the same for all individuals in the market.

A11. There are no transactions costs.

A12. Prices must adjust such that all securities are held by someone, i.e.,

$$\sum_{i=1}^{m} x_j^i = \sum_{i=1}^{m} \hat{x}_j^i = X_j \qquad j = 1, \ldots, n.$$

**4.2.1. Discussion of Assumptions.** The significant assumptions are A1, A3, A4, and A12. A1 restricts the analysis to a single-period model. Therefore, it precludes consideration of holding period effects and switching strategies.

Assumption A3 asserts that each individual maximizes the expected utility of his *future wealth*. The variable of the utility function has been made wealth and not returns. This decision has been made for two reasons: (1) When prices are allowed to vary, the wealth that an individual has available for investment is a variable that depends on the equilibrium level of prices. Making wealth the variable instead of returns makes this dependence on prices explicit. (2) The number of utility functions that are independent of the scale of investment are extremely limited.

Other than assuming that a utility function exists and that wealth is the relevant argument for the utility function, Assumption A3 places no other restrictions on the form of the utility function. Assumption A4, that an individual's risk function (either $\psi(x_1^i, \ldots, x_n^i)$ or $\phi(x_1^i, \ldots, x_n^i)$) is a continuous differentiable function of the $x_j^i$'s, imposes a continuity restriction on $U^i(W)$.

The analysis to be carried out in subsequent chapters will implicitly assume that the form of an individual's utility functions is such that if each of the set of individuals comprising the market acts subject to a wealth constraint to maximize his own utility function, then a market equilibrium solution exists. However, the assumption of a concave utility function is not made explicitly.

Note that individuals are allowed to have completely different utility functions; they are not constrained through the form of their utility function to agree on what constitutes the desirable properties of a portfolio of risky assets.

Implicit in the idea of *expected* utility is the assumption that the probability distribution of price expectations for each security can be combined to form a probability distribution for future wealth. Although such a procedure is computationally nontrivial, there are no theoretical barriers to this procedure.

The fact that individuals are viewed as entering the market with fixed probability distributions on future prices of securities means that all search and all interindividual communication has occurred. Individuals are now acting to maximize utility on the basis of given beliefs; there is no revision of probability distributions on the basis of the observed demand for securities. Current prices are assumed to convey information only about demand and supply and not about future performance of securities.

Assumption A12 is the market-clearing requirement for each security. It ensures that the supply and demand are equal for all securities. Assumptions A1 through A11 describe the asset-selection process of a "mathematized" individual in the environment of a highly simplified securities market. Assumption A12 transforms the asset-selection process into a model of market equilibrium. The asset-selection part of the model describes how individuals, having expectations about future prices and facing a *given* set of current security prices, will choose their portfolios. The market-clearing requirement of Assumption A12 ensures that the prices individuals face are the prices that will produce market equilibrium.

This distinction between simple asset selection and market equilibrium is formalized in the definitions given below.

DEFINITION 4.1. An individual is said to be in *personal equilibrium* when he has maximized his expected utility subject to his wealth constraint for any given set of prices.

DEFINITION 4.2. *Market equilibrium* is said to occur when (1) all individuals in the market are in personal equilibrium; and (2) prices are such that all markets are cleared. It is seen that market equilibrium implies personal equilibrium for all individuals in the market; however, personal equilibrium, even for all individuals, does not imply market equilibrium, because it does not ensure that demand and supply are equal for individual securities.

The assumption that individuals buy and sell at the same price is important when there exists a riskless asset. It means in effect that the borrowing and the lending rate must be the same.

The form of the wealth constraint is similar to that used by Mossin [19]. This formulation of the wealth constraint makes explicit the fact that securities are held by someone and that an individual's wealth depends on the current prices of the securities he holds.

This form of the wealth constraint assumes no margin requirement on short sales and allows short sales to generate capital for investing in long positions. Thus, selling short is a sort of "borrowing with risk." However, as long as one allows unlimited borrowing, the effect of margin requirements can be overcome by borrowing to put up the margin money for short sales. Thus, without assuming capital rationing, the imposition of margin requirements is not meaningful.

There are two views that can be taken of margin requirements: (1) The prices and return expected for a short position can be adjusted to take account of margin requirements; and (2) One can rewrite the wealth constraint as

$$\sum_{j=1}^{n} p_j |x_j| = \sum_{j=1}^{n} p_j |\hat{x}_j| = V_0$$

where absolute values replace the $x_j$. Neither of these approaches will be employed in this book.

The remaining assumptions have been made primarily for analytical simplicity to facilitate exposition of the material. The assumption of fractional shares and continuity of the risk function does not impose any significant loss of generality, but it does make the analysis amenable to the calculus. Similarly, the assumption that short sales are allowed, and that the number of shares are constant, has been made to simplify analysis. Dropping these assumptions would lead to inequality constraints, mathematical programing problems, and Kuhn–Tucker conditions. Although such problems can be formulated with ease, the extraction of meaningful results is difficult.

**4.2.2. Assumptions Not Made.** Having read the list of assumptions and the discussion of them, the reader is probably wondering how the term *general* is justified in the title. Part of the justification is the assumptions not made; the other part is the generality of the assumptions made.

It has *not* been assumed (1) that all investors have the same probability distribution for future prices or even attribute the same parameters to future price distributions such as the same mean and variance; (2) that all investors agree on the functional form of the measure of risk, i.e., that all investors regard some given parameter (such as variance or standard deviation) as the measure of risk; or (3) that there exists a riskless asset or if there is a riskless asset, that all investors regard the same asset as riskless.

Each of these three assumptions has been made in the models of Sharpe, Lintner, and Mossin in addition to more specific, albeit often not explicitly stated, forms of Assumptions A1 to A12. Each of these models assumes a single period, an underlying probabilistic structure to the formation of future expectations, the various simplifying perfect market assumptions, and finally, a mean-variance objective function.

Much of the generality of the model is contained in the representation of expected utility. Both the GMC and the TPFR are general risk-return formulations. Any allowable utility function of any continuous measure of risk can be represented as special cases of one (or both) of these two utility functions.

### 4.3. The Equilibrium Model

Having stated the basic assumptions, we shall now analyze the mathematical structure of the model. The model is analyzed with a general expression for expected utility before specializing to one of the two-parameter expressions in order to make explicit those results that arise simply in maximizing utility and those that arise from the two-parameter representations.

**4.3.1. Equilibrium Equations.** Let the expected value of utility for individual $i$, $E^i[U^i(W^i)]$ be denoted by $\overline{U}^i$. Form the Lagrangian $L^i$ for individual $i$ to maximize $\overline{U}^i$ subject to his wealth constraint:

$$L^i = \overline{U}^i(x_1^i, \ldots, x_n^i) - \lambda^i \sum_{j=1}^{n} p_j(x_j^i - \hat{x}_j^i),$$

where $\lambda^i$ is the Lagrange multiplier. The first-order conditions for each individual are

$$0 = \frac{\partial L^i}{\partial x_j^i} = \frac{\partial \overline{U}^i}{\partial x_j^i} - \lambda^i p_j \qquad \begin{matrix} i = 1, \ldots, m \\ j = 1, \ldots, n \end{matrix} \tag{4.1}$$

$$0 = \frac{\partial L^i}{\partial \lambda^i} = \sum_{j=1}^{n} p_j(x_j^i - \hat{x}_j^i) \qquad i = 1, \ldots, m. \tag{4.2}$$

There are $n + 1$ equations of personal equilibrium for each individual. When these equations are solved with the prices regarded as parameters, they yield an expression for $x_j^i$ as a function of prices and thus tell how many shares of each security each individual will buy at any given set of prices.

For determination of security prices at market equilibrium, the market clearing conditions must also be imposed.

The equilibrium equations and variables are summarized in Tables 4.1 and 4.2.

From these tables it is seen that the number of equations is equal to the number of variables, $mn + m + n$. For the values of all variables to be specified, the equations must be independent. However, independence does not hold. There are at most $mn + m + n - 1$ independent equations.

TABLE 4.1. SUMMARY OF MARKET EQUILIBRIUM EQUATIONS.

| Description of Equation | Typical Equation | Range | Number of Equations |
|---|---|---|---|
| First-order condition | $\dfrac{\partial \overline{U}}{\partial x_j^i} - \lambda^i p_j = 0$ | $i = 1, \ldots, m$<br>$j = 1, \ldots, n$ | $mn$ |
| Wealth constraint | $\displaystyle\sum_{j=1}^{n} p_j(x_j^i - \hat{x}_j^i) = 0$ | $i = 1, \ldots, m$ | $m$ |
| Market clearing | $\displaystyle\sum_{i=1}^{n} x_j^i = X_j$ | $j = 1, \ldots, n$ | $n$ |

TABLE 4.2. SUMMARY OF VARIABLES.

| Variable Type | Variable Symbol | Range | Number of Variables |
|---|---|---|---|
| Portfolio position | $x_j^i$ | $i = 1, \ldots, m$<br>$j = 1, \ldots, n$ | $mn$ |
| Lagrange multiplier | $\lambda^i$ | $i = 1, \ldots, m$ | $m$ |
| Security price | $p_j$ | $j = 1, \ldots, n$ | $n$ |

### 4.3.2. Redundancy of Equations

THEOREM 4.1. One of the $n + m$ market clearing equations and wealth constraint equations is redundant.

Two proofs of this theorem will be given.

PROOF 1. Assume that all $m$ wealth constraints are valid, but that only $n - 1$ of the market-clearing equations hold. It will be shown that these equations imply the $n$th market-clearing equation and, therefore, that the entire set of equations possesses a redundant equation. We rewrite the $m$ wealth constraints as

$$\sum_{j=1}^{n-1} p_j(x_j^i - \hat{x}_j^i) + p_n(x_n^i - \hat{x}_n^i) = 0 \qquad i = 1, \ldots, m.$$

Summing these equations over $i$ gives

$$\sum_{i=i}^{m} \sum_{j=1}^{n-1} p_j(x_j^i - \hat{x}_j^i) + p_n \sum_{i=i}^{m} (x_n^i - \hat{x}_n^i) = 0$$

$$\Rightarrow \sum_{j=1}^{n-1} \underbrace{\left( \sum_{i=1}^{m} x_j^i - \hat{x}_j^i \right)}_{\substack{\| \\ 0}} + p_n \sum_{i=1}^{m} (x_n^i - \hat{x}_n^i) = 0$$

by using the first $n - 1$ market-clearing conditions

$$\therefore \quad p_n \sum_{i=1}^{m} (x_n^i - \hat{x}_n^i) = 0$$

$$\Rightarrow \sum_{i=1}^{m} (x_n^i - \hat{x}_n^i) = 0 \quad \text{since} \quad p_n \neq 0.$$

Since the $m$ wealth constraints and $(n - 1)$ of the market clearing conditions imply the validity of the $n$th market-clearing condition, we conclude that one of the market clearing equations is redundant.

Q.E.D.

The purpose of the second proof is to show that the redundant equation can be a wealth constraint as well as a market clearing condition.

PROOF 2. Assume that all $n$ market-clearing conditions are valid, but that only the first $m - 1$ wealth constraints hold. It will now be shown that these equations imply the $m$th wealth constraint and are, therefore, redundant. We have the $n$ market-clearing equations

$$\sum_{i=1}^{m} (x_j^i - \hat{x}_j^i) = 0 \quad j = 1, \ldots, n \text{ by assumption.}$$

Multiplying by $p_j$ and summing over $j$ gives

$$p_j \sum_{i=1}^{m} (x_j^i - \hat{x}_j^i) = 0 \Rightarrow \sum_{j=1}^{n} \sum_{i=1}^{m} p_j(x_j^i - \hat{x}_j^i) = 0.$$

And rewriting this expression by changing the order of summation and grouping the first $(m - 1)$ terms gives

$$\sum_{i=1}^{m-1} \underbrace{\left( \sum_{j=1}^{n} p_j(x_j^i - \hat{x}_j^i) \right)}_{\substack{\| \\ 0}} + \sum_{j=1}^{n} p_j(x_j^m - \hat{x}_j^m) = 0.$$

The first term is zero, since we have assumed that the wealth constraint holds for the first $m - 1$ investors. Therefore, we have

$$\sum_{j=1}^{n} p_j(x_j^m - \hat{x}_j^m) = 0,$$

which is the wealth constraint for the $m$th individual.

Q.E.D.

We have given two proofs of the existence of a redundant equation in the sets of wealth constraints and market-clearing conditions in order to establish that the redundancy is not just the result of a redundant equation in the wealth constraints or just in the market-clearing conditions, but rather that it arises from combining the two sets of equations. This fact is established when it is shown that either set can have a redundant equation when the two are combined.

**4.3.3. Interpretation of the Lagrange Multiplier.** It is well known from the theory of constrained maximization that if some function is maximized subject to a single constraint, then the Lagrange multiplier is the rate of change of the function being maximized with respect to the constraint variable evaluated at the optimum point. Such an interpretation holds in the market equilibrium model *with conditions*.

THEOREM 4.2. The Lagrange multiplier $\lambda^i$ is the marginal utility of wealth for individual $i$ under the condition that prices are constant, i.e.,

$$\lambda^i = \left(\frac{\partial \bar{U}^i}{\partial V_0^i}\right)_\mathbf{p}, \tag{4.3}$$

where the subscript $\mathbf{p}$ on the derivative indicates that prices are held constant.

PROOF.

$$d\bar{U}^i = \sum_{j=1}^{n} \frac{\partial \bar{U}^i}{\partial x_j^i} dx_j^i$$

$$\frac{\partial \bar{U}^i}{\partial x_j^i} = \lambda^i p_j \text{ from Equation 4.1 of the first-order conditions}$$

$$\therefore \quad d\bar{U}^i = \lambda^i \sum_{j=1}^{n} p_j \, dx_j^i.$$

But the differential of wealth for individual $i$ *at constant prices* is

$$dV_0^i = \sum_{j=1}^{n} p_j dx_j^i$$

$$\Rightarrow \left(\frac{d\overline{U}^i}{dV_0^i}\right)_{\mathbf{p}} = \lambda^i, \tag{4.4}$$

where the subscript $\mathbf{p}$ on the derivative indicates that prices are held constant.

Q.E.D.

The fact that $\lambda^i$ is the marginal utility of wealth at constant prices and not simply the marginal utility of wealth arises from the fact that the individual, in maximizing his utility, is a "price taker" and does not regard prices as variable. The necessity to indicate explicitly that the differential of current wealth is

$$dV_0^i = \sum_{j=1}^{n} p_j dx_j^i$$

only at constant prices arises from the fact that prices are variables and not parameters in the context of the complete market-equilibrium model. Then $dV_0^i$ is given by

$$dV_0^i = \sum_{j=1}^{n} p_j \, dx_j^i + \sum_{j=1}^{n} dp_j x_j^i.$$

**4.3.4. Relative Prices.** In the theory of market equilibrium under conditions of certainty, it is well known that only relative and not absolute prices can be determined. Since mathematical expectation is a linear operator, replacing utility by expected utility in going to the theory of market equilibrium under conditions of risk should not alter the fact that only relative prices can be determined. The key to ascertaining that only relative prices are specified by the model is to show that the equilibrium equations are homogeneous of degree zero in prices. The market-clearing condition does not depend explicitly on prices; the wealth constraint is clearly homogeneous of degree zero in prices; therefore, the crucial equation for ascertaining homogeneity is

$$\frac{\partial \overline{U}^i}{\partial x_j^i} - \lambda^i p_j = 0.$$

It is not immediately clear whether or not this equation is homogeneous of degree zero in prices. The term $\partial \overline{U}^i / \partial x_j^i$ is not an explicit function of current prices;[1] hence, the equation will be homogeneous of degree zero in prices if and only if $\lambda^i p_j$ is homogeneous of degree zero in prices. We now give two proofs, one a brute-force derivation and the other a somewhat more sophisticated argument, that $\lambda^i p_j$ is homogeneous of degree zero in prices.

THEOREM 4.3. The term $\lambda^i p_j$ is homogeneous of degree zero in prices.

PROOF 1. Eliminate $\lambda^i$ from the first-order conditions of individual $i$ by solving the $n$th equation for $\lambda^i$ and substituting this solution into the remaining $n - 1$ first-order equations for individual $i$. We have

$$\frac{\partial \overline{U}^i}{\partial x_j^i} - \lambda^i p_j = 0 \qquad j = 1, \ldots, n$$

$$\Rightarrow \lambda^i = \frac{1}{p_n} \frac{\partial \overline{U}^i}{\partial x_n^i} \tag{4.5}$$

$$\Rightarrow \frac{\partial \overline{U}}{\partial x_j^i} - \frac{p_j}{p_n} \frac{\partial \overline{U}}{\partial x_n^i} = 0 \qquad j = 1, \ldots, n - 1. \tag{4.6}$$

Clearly, Equation 4.6 is homogeneous of degree zero in prices. Denoting the price ratio by

$$q_j \equiv \frac{p_j}{p_n}, \tag{4.7}$$

---

[1] To see that $\partial \overline{U}_i / \partial x_j^i$ is independent of prices, consider the following argument:

$$U^i(\widetilde{W}^i) = U\left( \sum_{j=1}^n \widetilde{\mu}_j^i x_j^i \right)$$

since

$$\widetilde{W}^i = \sum_{j=1}^n \widetilde{\mu}_j^i x_j^i$$

is future wealth of individual $i$.

We have

$$E^i[U^i(\widetilde{W}^i)] = \int \cdots \int_{\hat{\mu}} U^i\left( \sum_{j=1}^n \widetilde{\mu}_j^i x_j^i \right) dF^i(\widetilde{\mu}^i)$$

where $F(\hat{\mu}^i)$ is the probability distribution. Hence, future prices are "expected out" of the distribution; *present prices* never enter since neither $U^i(W^i)$ nor $dF^i(\hat{\mu}^i)$ are functions of current prices.

we have the following subset of equations:

$$\frac{\partial \overline{U}}{\partial x_j^i} - q_j \frac{\partial \overline{U}}{\partial x_n^i} = 0 \qquad \begin{array}{l} i = 1, \ldots, m \\ j = 1, \ldots, n-1 \end{array}$$

$$\sum_{j=1}^{n} q_j(x_j^i - \hat{x}_j^i) = 0 \qquad i = 1, \ldots, m \qquad (4.8)$$

$$\sum_{i=1}^{m} x_j^i = X_j \qquad j = 1, \ldots, n-1.$$

This is a set of $mn + n - 1$ independent equations (the $n$th market-clearing equation has been omitted as the redundant equation) in the $mn$ position variables $x_j^i$ and the $n - 1$ relative price variables $q_j$. (The $m$ Lagrange multipliers have been eliminated as well as $m$ of the first-order conditions.) Since this set of equations has relative prices as variables and not absolute prices, it is clearly homogeneous of degree zero in prices; moreover, since this set of equations will determine the equilibrium relative prices and since the remaining $m$ equations cannot lead to the specification of any absolute price, the initial system had to be homogeneous of degree zero in prices.

Q.E.D.

PROOF 2. From Equation 4.3 for $\lambda^i$, we have

$$\lambda^i = \left( \frac{\partial \overline{U}^i}{\partial V_0^i} \right)_{\mathbf{p}}.$$

Since $\overline{U}^i$ is independent of $\mathbf{p}$, and since

$$V_0^i = \sum_{j=1}^{n} p_j x_j^i$$

is homogeneous of degree 1 in $\mathbf{p} = (p_1, \ldots, p_n)$, we have $\lambda^i$ homogeneous of degree $-1$ in prices. Therefore, $\lambda^i p_j$ is homogeneous of degree zero in prices.

Q.E.D.

**4.3.5. Comparison of Consumer Choice and Portfolio Selection Models.** In the theory of consumer choice under certainty,[2] an individual is assumed to choose goods in order to maximize the certain utility of consumption subject to a wealth constraint. Letting

$$\begin{aligned} U(g_1, \ldots, g_n) &= \text{utility of goods purchased,} \\ g_j &= \text{quantity of good } j \text{ purchased,} \\ p_j &= \text{price of good } j, \text{ and} \\ W &= \text{wealth,} \end{aligned}$$

[2] See Samuelson [23], Chapter 5, for a treatment of consumer choice under certainty.

the consumer choice problem is to maximize $U(g_1, \ldots, g_n)$ such that $W = \sum_j p_j g_j$. The first-order conditions for maximization of utility subject to the wealth constraint, given a set of prices, are

$$\frac{dU}{dg_j} = \lambda p_j,$$

where $\lambda$ is again the Lagrange multiplier. This equation is structurally the same as the first-order condition for personal equilibrium given by Equation 4.1 in the capital-market equilibrium model. The difference is that individuals are choosing securities instead of goods, maximizing the *expected* utility of *uncertain* future wealth rather than the certain utility of a pattern of consumption. These distinctions are, however, conceptual, having to do only with the names of variables and possibly the complexity of the objective function; however, in terms of mathematical structure, the two problems are the same.

A distinction in the two problems arises when one assumes not simply that expected utility is a function of portfolio position, but that expected utility can be represented as a function of two parameters, future wealth and risk. Then, the theory of asset selection becomes a model for investigating the relation between return and risk, an entity which does not even exist in the theory of consumer choice under certainty.

When consumer choice is formulated in the context of an exchange market, it is generally assumed that consumers enter the market with a fixed endowment of goods and trading takes place. The result of trading is the determination of a set of relative prices that result in all markets being cleared. Again the logical structure of the equilibrium of an exchange market of consumer goods is similar to, albeit less complicated than, the structure of the capital-market equilibrium that has been formulated in this chapter. The preceding results on the existence of a redundant equation, the determination of relative prices, and the interpretation of the Lagrange multiplier have analogues in the theory of exchange-market equilibrium. These properties have been investigated with a general expected utility function instead of one of the two-parameter representations in order to make explicit that these are general properties of market equilibrium and are not dependent on the two-parameter representations. Now that these general features of the model have been established, we shall in subsequent chapters consider the general two-parameter functional representation and the generalized Markowitz criterion.

A major purpose of this work is the investigation of the relationship between return and risk in the context of market equilibrium. It is the representation of utility in terms of expected future wealth and risk that makes this analysis feasible. *The explicit introduction of risk as one argument of the expected utility function is the conceptual extension of the structure of the model beyond the traditional models of consumer choice.* This explicit treatment of the two-parameter objective functions is contained in Chapters 5 and 6. We begin the consideration of risk and return after making a further comment.

## 4.4. A Note on Consumption and Investment Selection

The preceding formulation of the investment-selection process has ignored the consumption decision of the investor. It has simply assumed that an investor enters the market at a certain time with an endowment $\hat{x}^i = (\hat{x}^i_1, \ldots, \hat{x}^i_n)$ of securities and invests the entire value of this endowment (including in the investment the possibility of holding cash). This formulation must assume either that the consumption decision is independent of the investment decision, or that the consumption decision will be ignored. The former approach postulates away the interdependence of the consumption and the investment decisions; the latter does not even bother to recognize the problem.

Neither approach is satisfactory. The fact is that the amount consumed will in general depend on the available investment opportunities, more being consumed when an individual regards these opportunities as poor.

The consumption decision can be incorporated within the portfolio-decision problem of the individual in the context of market equilibrium. The method is to create a set of dummy securities that contribute utility and have a cost, but no risk, associated with their purchase. Letting the $N$ consumption goods have price $p_j$ for amount $x_j$ for $j = n + 1, \ldots, N$, the wealth constraint becomes

$$\sum_{j=1}^{n} p_j(x_j - \hat{x}_j) + \sum_{j=n+1}^{n+N} p_j x_j = 0$$

or

$$\sum_{j=1}^{n+N} p_j x_j = \sum_{j=1}^{n} p_j \hat{x}_j = V_0$$

For the TPFR, expected utility would be $\overline{U} = f(\overline{W}, \psi, x_{n+1}, \ldots, x_{n+N})$. Thus, expected utility depends on expected future wealth, expected risk, and the consumption pattern. For any fixed consumption pattern, we have the case for which $\overline{U}$ depends on $\overline{W}$ and $\psi$ with an "effective initial endowment" of $V_0^*$ given by[3]

$$V_0^* = \sum_{j=1}^{n} p_j \hat{x}_j - \sum_{j=n+1}^{N} p_j x_j.$$

---

[3] The treatment is still artificial since it has not allowed for income, a flow variable; however, it is difficult to introduce flows in a single-period model.

In the market equilibrium context of the single-period portfolio problem, the consumption-investment decision can be regarded as an interdependent process in which current consumption is traded for the utility of expected future wealth depending on both an individual's expectations and the available opportunities. The available opportunities are determined by prices that are the result of the interaction of the utility functions and expectations of all individuals. This extension of the portfolio-selection process in the context of market equilibrium significantly increases the information requirements of individuals, the size of the problem, and the computational task (if an actual solution were to be attempted), but it requires no significant change in the logical structure of the problem. The broadening of the portfolio problem to include the joint consumption-investment problem is primarily a conceptual and not a structural change.

This joint treatment of the consumption-investment decision has structured the problem of how much of an individual's wealth will be invested in securities. This wealth is no longer exogenously specified. Hence, this reformulation of the model does achieve a conceptual clarification of the investment decision.

Having indicated that the single-period consumption decision can be incorporated within the framework of the model, we shall in the rest of this work proceed to refer to the individual's decision problem as a simple single-period investment decision with the understanding that the consumption decision can, if desired, be treated.

# 5
# Asset
# Selection
# and Market
# Equilibrium
# under a
# General
# Two-Parameter
# Functional
# Representation

The reader may assume about the two-parameter functional representation any of four attitudes that parallel the four possible uses of the theory developed in this chapter. These attitudes are (1) that whether or not the second parameter in the TPFR is a valid two-parameter representation of expected utility, the theory to be developed does describe the relations between return and this parameter that arise from maximizing expected utility; (2) that the two-parameter functional representation simply represents a generalization of the structure of the mean-variance models whose development is valuable for investigating these models or analogous models that use some property of the probability distribution as measures of risk; (3) that the TPFR is a more general version of the GMC that may be specialized to the GMC by properly choosing $f$ and $\psi$; and (4) that the TPFR is an alternative to the GMC when $\psi$ is defined to be $\pi$ and $f(W, \psi)$ is $U(\overline{W} - \pi)$.[1]

In this chapter we develop first-order conditions for personal equilibrium, derive an expression for the rate of substitution of risk for return, and investigate properties of personal equilibrium. We then develop a general first-order partial differential equation relating risk and return. This general equation is then specialized to the case of homogeneous risk functions and riskless assets. Attempts are made to relate portfolio return to portfolio risk, to assess the measure of risk for individual securities, and to relate the difference in return on the individual securities to security risk. The determination of equilibrium prices is considered and the steps involved in a solution are outlined.

Throughout, the analysis proceeds from the more general to the more specific. Simplifying assumptions are adduced only when needed. Great effort is made to make clear the role of a riskless asset, complete agreement, and homogeneous risk measures. Homogeneity of a risk measure is shown to be a very important simplifying property.

## 5.1. A Note on Variable Changes

When we speak of risk-return relationships, we shall mean either dollar

---

[1] See the end of Chapter 3 for a discussion of the relation of the GMC to the TPFR.

return $\overline{W}$ and its associated risk $\psi$ or relative return $\rho$ and its associated risk $\Psi$. The term *risk-return* may be used as a generic term for either relationship, or, depending on context, it may refer to one or the other.

Two different sets of variables will be used in the remainder of this book, and transformations from one set to another will occur frequently. The reader should master both sets and be able to change variables quickly.

Absolute variables are number of shares, share prices, total wealth, and total portfolio risk; relative variables are the relative wealth invested in securities, security returns, portfolio return, and risk per dollar. Listed below are the relative variables and their relation to the absolute variables. (Cf. Section 4.1.3 for a complete listing of variables and their definitions.)

$$y_j = \frac{p_j x_j}{V_0} = \text{relative investment in security } j$$

$$r_j = \frac{\mu_j}{p_j} - 1 - \text{return in security } j$$

$$\rho = \frac{W - V_0}{V_0} = \text{portfolio return}$$

$$\Phi = \frac{\phi}{V_0} = \text{risk per dollar in the GMC}$$

$$\Psi = \frac{\psi}{V_0} = \text{risk per dollar in the TPFR.}$$

## 5.2. A Note on Measures of Risk

In this chapter a number of measures of risk will be used. The purpose of this note is to state the various definitions of risk and their notation, to show their relation, and especially to show that the two expressions for marginal risk are consistently defined.

$$\psi^i(x_1^i, \ldots, x_n^i) = \text{total portfolio risk for individual } i$$

$$\Psi^i \equiv \frac{\psi^i}{V_0^i} = \text{portfolio risk per dollar for individual } i$$

$$\psi_j^i \equiv \left(\frac{\partial \psi^i}{\partial x_j^i}\right)_{\mathbf{p}} = \text{marginal portfolio risk of security } j \text{ for individual } i \text{ at constant prices}$$

$$\Psi_j^i = \frac{1}{p_j}\left(\frac{\partial \psi^i}{\partial x_j^i}\right)_{\mathbf{p}} = \text{"marginal risk per dollar" for security } j \text{ for individual } i \text{ at constant prices.}$$

LEMMA 5.1. $\Psi^i_j$, the marginal risk per dollar for security $j$, is given by either

$$\left(\frac{\partial \Psi^i}{\partial y^i_j}\right)_{\mathbf{p}} \quad \text{or} \quad \frac{1}{p_j}\left(\frac{\partial \psi^i}{\partial x^i_j}\right)_{\mathbf{p}}$$

where the price vector $\mathbf{p}$ on the derivatives indicates that prices are held constant.

PROOF.

$$\left(\frac{\partial \Psi^i}{\partial y^i_j}\right)_{\mathbf{p}} = \sum_{k=1}^{n} \frac{\partial(\psi^i/V^i_0)}{\partial x^i_k}\left(\frac{\partial x^i_k}{\partial y^i_j}\right)_{\mathbf{p}} = \frac{1}{V^i_0}\sum_{k=1}^{n}\left(\frac{\partial \psi^i}{\partial x^i_k}\right)_{\mathbf{p}}\frac{V^i_0}{p_k}\delta_{jk},$$

$$\text{since } x^i_k = \frac{V^i_0 y^i_k}{p_k} \Rightarrow \left(\frac{\partial x^i_k}{\partial y^i_j}\right)_{\mathbf{p}} = \frac{V^i_0}{p_k}\delta_{jk}$$

where $\delta_{jk}$ is the Kronecker delta.

$$\therefore \quad \left(\frac{\partial \Psi^i}{\partial y^i_j}\right)_{\mathbf{p}} = \frac{1}{p_j}\left(\frac{\partial \psi^i}{\partial x^i_j}\right)_{\mathbf{p}} = \Psi^i_j.$$

Q.E.D.

### 5.3. Equilibrium Equations

The equilibrium equations for the two-parameter functional representation are a special case of the equilibrium equations developed in Chapter 4 for the general case of any expected utility function. The representation of expected utility in terms of risk and return is a powerful tool for investigating asset selection and market equilibrium under conditions of uncertainty.

Let the expected utility of individual $i$ be of the form $f^i(W^i, \psi^i)$. Form the Lagrangian function[2]

$$L^i \equiv f^i(W^i, \psi^i) - \lambda^i\left[\sum_{j=1}^{n} p_j(x^i_j - \hat{x}^i_j)\right] \tag{5.1}$$

to reflect the wealth constraint of individual $i$ where $\lambda^i$ is the Lagrange multiplier.

The first-order conditions for maximization of Equation 5.1 are[3]

$$0 = \frac{\partial L^i}{\partial x^i_j} = \frac{\partial f^i}{\partial W^i}\frac{\partial W^i}{\partial x^i_j} + \frac{\partial f^i}{\partial \psi^i}\frac{\partial \psi^i}{\partial x^i_j} - \lambda^i p_j \tag{5.2}$$

---

[2] Throughout this chapter wealth $W$ will mean expected wealth. If the random variable is referred to, it will always have a tilde over it.
[3] This analysis does not assume that $\psi$ is an explicit function of $W$ but only that $\psi$ depends on $\mathbf{x}$ although this dependence could be via a dependence on $W$. This assumption will in no way change the results to be derived.

$$0 = \frac{\partial L^i}{\partial \lambda^i} = \sum_j p_j(x_j^i - \hat{x}_j^i).$$ (5.3)

These equations hold for every $i$ and for every $j$.

To simplify analysis, let us define the following notation:

$$\frac{\partial f^i}{\partial W^i} = f_1^i \qquad \frac{\partial f^i}{\partial \psi^i} = f_2^i \qquad \frac{\partial \psi^i}{\partial x_j^i} = \psi_j^i = \text{marginal risk of security } j.$$

Then, the equilibrium conditions can be expressed as

$$f_1^i \mu_j^i + f_2^i \psi_j^i = \lambda^i p_j \qquad \begin{matrix} i = 1, \ldots, m \\ j = 1, \ldots, n \end{matrix}$$ (5.4)

$$\sum_{j=1}^{n} p_j(x_j^i - \hat{x}_j^i) = 0 \qquad i = 1, \ldots, m$$ (5.5)

$$\sum_{i=1}^{n} x_j^i = X_j \qquad j = 1, \ldots, n-1,$$

where the market-clearing requirement has been added to the first-order conditions for personal equilibrium.

## 5.4. General Properties of Personal Equilibrium

THEOREM 5.1. At personal equilibrium the rate of substitution of risk for return for individual $i$ possessing an expected utility of wealth function $f^i(W^i, \psi^i)$ is given by

$$\frac{d\psi^i}{dW^i} = \frac{-f_1^i}{f_2^i} = \frac{\psi_j^i - (p_j/p_n)\psi_n^i}{\mu_j^i - (p_j/p_n)\mu_n^i} = \frac{\psi_j^i - q_j\psi_n^i}{\mu_j^i - q_j\mu_n^i}$$ (5.6)

where security $n$ has been chosen as a "reference security" and the relative price of security $j$ to security $n$ has been denoted by $q_j = p_j/p_n$.

PROOF. From Equation 5.4 we have

$$f_1^i \mu_j^i + f_2^i \psi_n^i = \lambda^i p_j \qquad j = 1, \ldots, n.$$

Solving the $n$th equation for $\lambda^i$ gives

$$\lambda^i = \frac{f_1^i \mu_n^i + f_2^i \psi_j^i}{p_n}.$$ (5.7)

Substituting this expression for $\lambda$ into the original equations and simplifying gives

$$f^i_1\left(\mu^i_j - \mu^i_n\frac{p_j}{p_n}\right) + f^i_2\left(\psi^i_j - \psi^i_n\frac{p_j}{p_n}\right) = 0 \qquad j = 1,\ldots,n-1$$

$$\Rightarrow \frac{d\psi^i}{dW^i} = \frac{-f^i_1}{f^i_2} = \frac{\psi^i_j - \psi^i_n(p_j/p_n)}{\mu^i_j - \mu^i_j(p_j/p_n)}.$$

Q.E.D.

Observe that the rate of substitution for individual $i$ depends only on the relative and not the absolute prices. Selecting security $n$ as the reference security has meant using the $n$th first-order equation to eliminate $\lambda^i$. Any other security could serve as the reference security just as easily.

There is some ambiguity in the term *risk premium*. In Chapter 3 we used the (dollar) risk premium $\pi$ which was the difference in the distribution mean $\overline{W}$ and the certainty equivalent $CE$. In the context of Chapter 3, $\pi$ was measured in dollars and related to the entire portfolio rather than to individual securities. It did not require a riskless asset to be well defined.[4]

DEFINITION 5.1. The *return risk premium* on a portfolio of risky assets, in the case in which there is a riskless asset, will be defined to be the difference in portfolio return $\rho$ and the return on the riskless asset $r_n$.

DEFINITION 5.2. The *relative risk premium* on securities $j$ and $k$ will be the difference in their returns, i.e., $r_j - r_k$.

LEMMA 5.2. If there exists a riskless asset, then the relative risk premium of two risky securities will equal the difference in their risk premium, i.e.,

$$r_j - r_k = m_j - m_k. \tag{5.8}$$

PROOF. Let $n$ be the riskless asset with return $r_n$ and let $m_j$ and $m_k$ be the return risk premium for securities $j$ and $k$. Then

$$r_j - r_k = (r_j - r_n) - (r_k - r_n) = m_j - m_k.$$

Q.E.D.

Lemma 5.2 establishes that the concept of relative risk premium is a generalization of the idea of comparing the difference in security risk premiums when there is a riskless asset. It shows that relative risk premium is well defined when there is a riskless asset.

---

[4] See Section 6.2.1., "Ambiguity in the Term *Risk Premium*," for a discussion of the relation between the dollar risk premium $\pi$, a measure of risk, and the return risk premium, $\rho - r_n$, a difference in returns.

DEFINITION 5.3. The *relative marginal risk* between securities $j$ and $k$ will be the difference in marginal risk for securities $j$ and $k$, i.e.,

$$\psi_j^i - \psi_k^i = \text{relative marginal risk.}$$

The term relative can be used in two ways: to indicate a ratio or a difference. We have defined relative risk premium and relative marginal risk to denote a *difference* and not a ratio. These two concepts will facilitate the generalization of the results for the case in which there is no riskless asset.

COROLLARY 5.1.1. The rate of substitution of risk for return can be expressed as the ratio of the difference in marginal risk per dollar and the return on any two distinct securities, i.e.,

$$\frac{d\psi^i}{dW^i} = \frac{\Psi_j^i - \Psi_n^i}{r_j^i - r_n^i}. \tag{5.9}$$

PROOF. From Equation 5.6 we have

$$\frac{d\psi^i}{dW^i} = \frac{\psi_j^i - \psi_n^i(p_j/p_n)}{\mu_j^i - \mu_n^i(p_j/p_n)}$$

$$\frac{d\psi^i}{dW^i} = \frac{\psi_j^i/p_j - \psi_n^i/p_n}{\mu_j^i/p_j - \mu_n^i/p_n}. \tag{5.10}$$

Since $1 + r_j^i \equiv \mu_j^i/p_j$ and $\psi_j^i/p_j \equiv \Psi_j^i$, Equation 5.10 becomes

$$\frac{d\psi^i}{dW^i} = \frac{\Psi_j^i - \Psi_n^i}{r_j^i - r_n^i}.$$

Q.E.D.

Note that Corollary 5.1.1 holds for *any* choice of $j$ and $n$ since the choice of security $n$ as the reference security in Equation 5.6 was completely arbitrary. This corollary asserts that $d\psi^i/dW^i$ is the ratio of relative marginal risk per dollar to relative risk premium.

COROLLARY 5.1.2. For any individual in personal equilibrium and for any choice of reference security, the ratio of the difference in marginal risk per dollar and the difference in return is the same for all securities, i.e.,

$$\frac{\Psi_j^i - \Psi_n^i}{r_j^i - r_n^i} = \frac{\Psi_k^i - \Psi_n^i}{r_k^i - r_n^i} \qquad j, k = 1, \ldots, n - 1. \tag{5.11}$$

PROOF. Let $n$ be the reference security. Then from Equation 5.9 we have

$$\frac{d\psi^i}{dW^i} = \frac{\Psi_j^i - \Psi_n^i}{r_j^i - r_n^i} \qquad j = 1, \ldots, n - 1.$$

Since the left-hand side is independent of the subscript $j$, we have

$$\frac{\Psi_j^i - \Psi_n^i}{r_j^i - r_n^i} = \frac{\Psi_k^i - \Psi_n^i}{r_k^i - r_n^i} \qquad j, k = 1, \ldots, n-1.$$

Q.E.D.

Thus we have shown that any individual chooses securities in such a fashion that all securities have the same ratio of relative marginal risk per dollar to relative risk premium at personal equilibrium. Since this holds for personal equilibrium, it holds for any set of prices that an individual faces.

LEMMA 5.3. For every individual we have

$$\left(\frac{d\psi^i}{dW^i}\right)_{\mathbf{p}} = \left(\frac{d\Psi^i}{d\rho^i}\right)_{\mathbf{p}}, \tag{5.12}$$

i.e., the rate of substitution of total portfolio risk for expected future wealth is equal to the rate of substitution of total portfolio risk per dollar for expected return *at constant prices*.

PROOF. By definition we have

$$\Psi^i \equiv \frac{\psi^i}{V_0^i} = \text{total portfolio risk per dollar}$$

$$\rho^i \equiv \sum_{j=1}^{n} r_j^i y_j^i = \text{expected portfolio return} \tag{5.13}$$

$$y_j^i \equiv \frac{p_j x_j^i}{V_0^i} = \text{relative wealth invested in security } j, \tag{5.14}$$

where $V_0^i = \sum_{j=1}^{n} p_j \hat{x}_j^i$ is individual $i$'s initial endowment of wealth at prices $\mathbf{p} = (p_1, \ldots, p_n)$. Therefore, the total differential for $\psi^i$ and $\rho^i$ at constant prices will be given by

$$(d\Psi^i)_{\mathbf{p}} = \frac{d\psi^i}{V_0^i}, \tag{5.15}$$

since $V_0^i$ is constant when $\mathbf{p}$ is constant and

$$(d\rho^i)_{\mathbf{p}} = \sum_{j=1}^{n} r_j^i (dy_j^i)_{\mathbf{p}} = \sum_{j=1}^{n} (1 + r_j^i)(dy_j^i)_{\mathbf{p}}, \tag{5.16}$$

since $\sum_{j=1}^{n} (dy_j^i)_{\mathbf{p}} = 0.$

Substituting $(dy_j^i)_\mathbf{p} = (p_j/V_0^i)\,dx_j^i$ into Equation 5.16 gives

$$(d\rho^i)_\mathbf{p} = \sum_{j=1}^{n} (1 + r_j^i)\frac{p_j}{V_0^i}\,dx_j^i$$

$$= \frac{1}{V_0^i}\sum_{j=1}^{n} \mu_j^i\,dx_j^i = \frac{dW^i}{V_0^i}. \tag{5.17}$$

From Equations 5.15 and 5.17 we have

$$\left(\frac{d\Psi^i}{d\rho^i}\right)_\mathbf{p} = \left(\frac{d\psi^i}{dW^i}\right)_\mathbf{p}.$$

Q.E.D.

Lemma 5.3 is valid for any values of the variables at any *given* set of prices. Unlike the theorems and corollaries being developed, its validity is not restricted to the point of personal equilibrium. Note that holding prices constant was a crucial element of the proof of Lemma 5.3. If prices were not held constant the relation between $d\psi^i/dW^i$ and $d\psi^i/d\rho^i$ would be quite complicated. This simple relation is important in our analysis of personal equilibrium because each individual decision-maker is assumed to be a price-taker. Thus, all relations for the rate of substitution of total portfolio risk for expected future wealth have an analogue in the rate of substitution of portfolio risk per dollar for expected return. This fact is convenient since both Sharpe and Lintner have formulated their models in terms of return and its variance, and not expected future wealth.

COROLLARY 5.1.3. At personal equilibrium,

$$\frac{d\Psi^i}{d\rho^i} = \frac{\Psi_j^i - \Psi_n^i}{r_j^i - r_n^i} \qquad \text{for every } i, j, n, \text{ such that } j \neq n. \tag{5.18}$$

PROOF. From Equation 5.9 of Corollary 5.1.1, we have

$$\frac{d\psi^i}{dW^i} = \frac{\Psi_j^i - \Psi_n^i}{r_j^i - r_n^i}$$

$$\Rightarrow \frac{d\Psi^i}{d\rho^i} = \frac{\Psi_j^i - \Psi_n^i}{r_j^i - r_n^i} \qquad \text{from Lemma 5.3.}$$

Q.E.D.

This corollary relates the rate of substitution of risk per dollar for expected return on the portfolio to the marginal risk per dollar and expected return on individual securities.

To summarize, we have obtained the following equivalent expressions for the rate of substitution of risk for return

$$\frac{d\psi^i}{dW^i} = \frac{\psi_j^i - q_j^i\psi_n^i}{\mu_j^i - q_j^i\mu_n^i} = \frac{d\Psi^i}{d\rho^i} = \frac{\Psi_j^i - \Psi_n^i}{r_j^i - r_n^i} \qquad j = 1, \ldots, n-1.$$

This set of equations, along with the wealth constraint, defines the personal equilibrium for individual $i$.

**5.4.1. The Measure of Security Risk.** Two important issues are (1) What is the proper measure of risk of an individual security? and (2) What determines the relative risk premium for a security? These two questions are clearly not independent. The answer to either depends on the measure of portfolio risk.

We are now in a position to answer these two questions in the context of the two-parameter functional representation of expected utility. Since the TPFR contains the GMC and the Sharpe, Lintner, and Mossin models, we will thus be answering the question for each of these models.

From Corollary 5.1.2 we saw that all portfolios must have the same ratio of relative marginal risk per dollar to relative return. *This result suggests that the proper measure of risk for an individual security is the marginal portfolio risk of that security.* It is not the absolute value of the marginal risk, but rather the size of the marginal risk when compared with some reference security. Hence, it is concluded that *the appropriate measure of risk for an individual security is the relative (in the sense of a difference) marginal portfolio risk.*

The use of marginal risk as the measure of security risk is quite meaningful for the following reasons. (1) The marginal criterion of risk asserts that the important thing about a security is the contribution to the portfolio risk of the last (infinitesimal fraction of a) share purchased. (2) It emphasizes that the important property of an individual security is its effect on the portfolio, and that security risk cannot be meaningfully defined independent of the portfolio choice process; hence, security risk is dependent on the properties of other securities in the market. (3) It is consistent with the extensive use of marginal criteria in decision-making under conditions of certainty. (4) Its use provides a natural, meaningful explanation for the difference in return on two securities. This last fact is established in the next corollary.

COROLLARY 5.1.4. The difference in return expected by any individual for any two securities is the product of the rate of substitution of expected portfolio return for portfolio risk per dollar times the difference in marginal risk for two securities, if there is a one-to-one relation between risk and return,[5] i.e.,

[5] This is a general expression for the so-called "market line" of the mean-variance models of market equilibrium. It is general because it does not assume a mean-variance formulation, a riskless asset, or complete agreement among investors. Moreover, the

$$r_j - r_n = \left(\frac{d\rho^i}{d\Psi^i}\right)_{\mathbf{p}} (\Psi^i_j - \Psi^i_n) \qquad \text{for every } i, j, n. \tag{5.19}$$

PROOF. The proof is straightforward. Solving Equation 5.18 for $r_j - r_n$ gives

$$r_j - r_n = \frac{\Psi^i_j - \Psi^i_n}{(d\Psi^i/d\rho^i)_{\mathbf{p}}} = \left(\frac{d\rho^i}{d\Psi^i}\right)_{\mathbf{p}} (\Psi^i_j - \Psi^i_n),$$

since

$$\left(\frac{d\Psi^i}{d\rho^i}\right)_{\mathbf{p}} = \left(\frac{d\rho^i}{d\Psi^i}\right)_{\mathbf{p}}^{-1},$$

when there is a one-to-one relation between $\Psi^i$ and $\rho^i$.

Q.E.D.

We now have an expression for the difference in return on two securities. The difference is proportional to the difference in security risk, i.e., the difference in marginal portfolio risk per dollar for the two securities. For any individual, the proportionality factor is the same for every pair of securities. The proportionality factor is simply the rate of substitution of expected return for portfolio risk. Thus, the structure of Equation 5.19 is exceedingly simple. It says

$$\Delta(\text{return}) = \frac{d(\text{return})}{d(\text{risk})} \Delta(\text{risk}), \tag{5.20}$$

where the symbol $\Delta$ denotes a difference and $d$ is the differential operator. Thus the difference in return on any two securities is the difference in risk times the rate of exchange of return for risk. *This rate of exchange is the value at personal equilibrium for each individual.*

Since Equation 5.19 is a personal equilibrium equation, it holds for any set of prices and not necessarily only for those that clear the market. Since personal equilibrium is a necessary condition for market equilibrium, it *is necessary* that Equation 5.19 hold in order to have market equilibrium, but that 5.19 hold *is not sufficient* for market equilibrium, since it holds for every set of prices with which an individual is confronted if he is in personal equilibrium.

---

fact that Equation 5.19 is a personal-equilibrium relationship indicates that "market line" is a misnomer. Equation 5.19 is valid when there is not market equilibrium and when the market line is not even well defined because of a lack of complete agreement. (If there is not complete agreement among investors, the idea of a return or risk expected by the market is not well defined.) Thus, the applicability of Equation 5.19, even in the special case of a mean-variance model, is more general than is indicated in the existing literature. This point will be pursued further in Chapters 7 and 8.

Note that neither the explicit result of Equation 5.19 nor the structural reexpression contained in Equation 5.20 have required the existence of a riskless asset or complete agreement.

Implicit in Equation 5.19 is a set of prices. For a different set of prices, one will usually obtain a different rate of exchange and a different value of marginal risk. *For Equation 5.19 to be a valid market-equilibrium relationship, one must evaluate the variables at each individual's position of personal equilibrium when he is confronted with a set of prices which clear the market.*

The fact that individuals with different expectations will assign different values to the variables in Equation 5.19 means that the solution implicit in this relationship will be different for each individual and, therefore, that neither the capital market line nor the market portfolio are well defined as the terms are used in the current literature.

We now return to the development of general theorems on the rate of substitution of risk for return.

**5.4.2. Weighted Averages and the Rate of Substitution of Risk for Return.** In this section we shall formulate weighted averages of marginal risk and relate them to the rate of substitution. These results, in addition to being interesting themselves, will establish the foundations for the study of the special class of homogeneous risk functions and for the investigation of the relation of portfolio return to portfolio risk.

THEOREM 5.2. The rates of exchange $d\psi^i/dW^i$ and $d\Psi^i/d\rho^i$ are related to the weighted marginal portfolio risk by

$$\frac{d\Psi^i}{d\rho^i} = \frac{\sum_{j=1}^{n} \Psi^i_j y^i_j - \Psi^i_n}{\rho^i - r^i_n} \tag{5.21}$$

and

$$\frac{d\psi^i}{dW^i} = \frac{\sum_{j=1}^{n} \psi^i_j x^i_j - (\psi^i_n/p_n)V^i_0}{W^i - (1 + r^i_n)V^i_0}, \tag{5.22}$$

where

$$\sum_{j=1}^{n} \psi^i_j x^i_j = \text{weighted marginal portfolio risk, and}$$

$$\sum_{j=1}^{n} \psi^i_j y^i_j = \text{weighted marginal portfolio risk per dollar.}$$

Note that the weights are the number of shares held for marginal portfolio risk and relative investment for marginal risk per dollar. Thus, each marginal risk is weighted by the portfolio position; the sum is then a weighted average of the risks of the individual securities. The $\{y_j^i\}$ are normalized weights; the $\{x_j^i\}$ are not.

PROOF. 1. To show $\dfrac{d\Psi^i}{d\rho^i} = \dfrac{\sum\limits_j \Psi_j^i y_j^i - \Psi_n^i}{\rho^i - r_n^i}$. From Equation 5.18,

$$\frac{d\Psi^i}{d\rho^i} = \frac{\Psi_j^i - \Psi_n^i}{r_j^i - r_n^i} \qquad j = 1,\ldots,n-1.$$

Multiplying numerator and denominator by $y_j^i$ gives

$$\frac{d\Psi^i}{d\rho^i} = \frac{\Psi_j^i y_j^i - \Psi_n^i y_j^i}{r_j^i y_j^i - r_n^i y_j^i}. \tag{A}$$

Applying the method of ratio addition[6] gives

$$\frac{d\Psi^i}{d\rho^i} = \frac{\sum\limits_{j=1}^{n-1} \Psi_j^i y_j^i - \Psi_n^i \sum\limits_{j=1}^{n-1} y_j^i}{\sum\limits_{j=1}^{n-1} r_j^i y_j^i - r_n^i \sum\limits_{j=1}^{n-1} y_j^i}.$$

The sum can go only to $(n-1)$ since Equation (A) holds only for $j = 1,\ldots,$ $n-1$. However, by adding and subtracting $\Psi_n^i y_n^i$ to both terms in the numerator and $r_n^i y_n^i$ to both terms in the denominator, one obtains

$$\frac{d\Psi^i}{d\rho^i} = \frac{\sum\limits_{j=1}^{n} \Psi_j^i y_n^i - \Psi_n^i \sum\limits_{j=1}^{n} y_j^i}{\sum\limits_{j=1}^{n} r_j^i y_j^i - r_n^i \sum\limits_{j=1}^{n} y_j^i} = \frac{\sum\limits_{j=1}^{n} \Psi_j^i y_j^i - \Psi_n^i}{\rho^i - r_n^i}$$

[6] The method of ratio addition asserts that if $y = a_i/b_i$ for $i = 1, \ldots, k$, then

$$y = \frac{\sum\limits_{i=1}^{k} a_i}{\sum\limits_{i=1}^{k} b_i}.$$

To prove this result is straightforward.

$$y = \frac{a_i}{b_i} \Rightarrow y b_i = a_i \Rightarrow y \sum_{i=1}^{k} b_i = \sum_{i=1}^{k} a_i$$

$$\Rightarrow y = \frac{\sum\limits_{i=1}^{k} a_i}{\sum\limits_{i=1}^{k} b_i}.$$

Q.E.D.

since

$$\sum_{j=1}^{n} y_j^i = 1 \text{ and } \rho^i = \sum_{j=1}^{n} r_j^i y_j^i.$$

2. To show $\dfrac{d\Psi^i}{dW^i} = \dfrac{\sum_{j=1}^{n} \Psi_j^i x_j^i - (\Psi_n^i / p_n) V_0^i}{W^i - (1 + r_n^i) V_0^i}.$     From Equation 5.6,

$$\frac{d\psi^i}{dW^i} = \frac{\psi_j^i - q_j \psi_n^i}{\mu_j^i - q_j \mu_n^i} \qquad j = 1, \ldots, n - 1.$$

Multiplying numerator and denominator by $x_j^i$ gives

$$\frac{d\psi^i}{dW^i} = \frac{\psi_j^i x_j^i - \psi_n^i q_j x_j^i}{\mu_j^i x_j^i - \mu_n^i q_j x_j^i} \qquad j = 1, \ldots, n - 1.$$

Using the method of ratio addition gives

$$\frac{d\psi^i}{dW^i} = \frac{\sum_{j=1}^{n-1} \psi_j^i x_j^i - \psi_n^i \sum_{j=1}^{n-1} q_j x_j^i}{\sum_{j=1}^{n-1} \mu_j^i x_j^i - \mu_n^i \sum_{j=1}^{n-1} q_j x_j^i}.$$

Adding and subtracting $\psi_n^i x_n^i$ to numerator and $\mu_n^i x_n^i$ to the denominator, we have

$$\frac{d\psi^i}{dW^i} = \frac{\sum_{j=1}^{n} \psi_j^i x_j^i - \psi_n^i \sum_{j=1}^{n} q_j x_j^i}{\sum_{j=1}^{n} \mu_j^i x_j^i - \mu_n^i \sum_{j=1}^{n} q_j x_j^i} = \frac{\sum_{j=1}^{n} \psi_j^i x_j^i - (\psi_n^i / p_n) V_0^i}{W^i - (1 + r_n^i) V_0^i}$$

since

$$\sum_{j=1}^{n} q_j x_j^i = \frac{V_0^i}{p_n} \qquad W^i = \sum_{j=1}^{n} \mu_j^i x_j^i \qquad 1 + r_n^i = \frac{\mu_n^i}{p_n}$$

Q.E.D.

Note that the wealth constraint was used explicitly in the derivation of both Equations 5.21 and 5.22. The previous expressions for the rate of substitution of risk for return had employed only the first $n$ of the $(n + 1)$ equations of personal equilibrium and had not used the wealth constraint. Thus, in the sense of depending on all of the equations of personal equilibrium, these two equations have more information content.

In the proof, Equations 5.21 and 5.22 were each derived from basic relations. One can present a shorter, but somewhat less instructional, proof of either one of the equations from the other by changing variables. We shall show that Equation 5.22 implies Equation 5.21.

COROLLARY 5.2.1. Equation 5.22 $\Rightarrow$ Equation 5.21.

PROOF. $\dfrac{d\psi^i}{dW^i} = \dfrac{d\Psi^i}{d\rho^i}$ by Lemma 5.3

$\therefore$ Equation 5.22 $\Rightarrow \dfrac{d\Psi^i}{d\rho^i} = \dfrac{\sum\limits_{j} \psi_j^i x_j^i - (\psi_n^i/p_n)V_0^i}{W^i - (1 + r_n^i)V_0^i}.$

Dividing by $V_0^i$ gives

$$\dfrac{d\Psi^i}{d\rho^i} = \dfrac{\sum\limits_{j=1}^{n} (\psi_j^i/p_j)[(p_j x_j^i)/(V_0^i)] - \psi_n^i/p_n}{(W^i - V_0^i)/(V_0^i) - r_n^i} = \dfrac{\sum\limits_{j=1}^{n} \Psi_j^i y_j^i - \Psi_n^i}{\rho^i - r_n^i}.$$

Q.E.D.

The key in this proof has been in transforming $x_j^i$ into $y_j^i$, $W^i$ into $\rho^i$, and $\psi_j^i$ into $\Psi_j^i$. One can, by working backward, prove that Equation 5.21 implies Equation 5.22. This proof will not be given here.

In interpreting Theorem 5.2, we shall limit discussion to Equation 5.21. The term $\sum\limits_{j=1}^{n} \Psi_j^i y_j^i$ is a normalized weighting of the expected marginal risk per dollar on each security by the relative investment in each security. Thus the numerator is the weighted marginal risk minus the comparable risk of the arbitrary reference security. The denominator is the expected return on the portfolio minus the reference return. Thus the result still has the structure of

$$\frac{d\,(\text{risk})}{d\,(\text{return})} = \frac{\text{weighted marginal risk} - \text{reference risk}}{\text{portfolio return} - \text{reference return}}. \tag{5.23}$$

However, previously the risk and return were values for individual securities (cf. Equations 5.19 and 5.20); now the risk is a weighted average and the return is the portfolio return itself. We shall shortly investigate under what conditions the weighted risk can be replaced by a function of portfolio risk itself.

All of the preceding expressions for the rate of substitution for both risk and return have involved a reference security. The way the reference security enters the results is the process of eliminating the Lagrange multiplier from the equations (see the proof of Theorem 5.1 and especially Equation 5.7) The equation to be derived in Theorem 5.3 does not involve a reference security because it does not directly eliminate $\lambda$ from the problem.

THEOREM 5.3. The rate of substitution of risk for return for individual $i$ at personal equilibrium is given by

$$\frac{d\psi^i}{dW^i} = \frac{\sum_{j=1}^{n} \psi_j^i(x_j^i - \hat{x}_j^i)}{\sum_{j=1}^{n} \mu_j^i(x_j^i - \hat{x}_j^i)}, \tag{5.24}$$

where $\mathbf{x}^i = (x_1^i, \ldots, x_n^i)$ and $\hat{\mathbf{x}}^i = (\hat{x}_1^i, \ldots, \hat{x}_n^i)$ are individual $i$'s equilibrium portfolio and initial endowment, respectively.

PROOF. Solving Equation 5.4 for $p_j$ and substituting this expression for $p_j$ into Equation 5.5, one obtains

$$p_j = \frac{f_1^i \mu_j^i + f_2^i \psi_j^i}{\lambda^i}$$

$$\Rightarrow 0 = \sum_{j=1}^{n} p_j(x_j^i - \hat{x}_j^i) = \sum_{j=1}^{n} (f_1^i \mu_j^i + f_2^i \psi_j^i)(x_j^i - \hat{x}_j^i)$$

$$\Rightarrow f_1^i \left[ \sum_{j=1}^{n} \mu_j^i(x_j^i - \hat{x}_j^i) \right] = -f_2^i \left[ \sum_{j=1}^{n} \psi_j^i(x_j^i - \hat{x}_j^i) \right]$$

$$\Rightarrow \frac{d\psi^i}{dW^i} = \frac{-f_1^i}{f_2^i} = \frac{\sum_{j=1}^{n} \psi_j^i(x_j^i - \hat{x}_j^i)}{\sum_{j=1}^{n} \mu_j^i(x_j^i - \hat{x}_j^i)}.$$

Q.E.D.

In this expression the wealth constraint was used explicitly; this was the means by which solving for the Lagrange multiplier was avoided.

This expression for the rate of substitution is again a ratio of weighted averages. The expressions appear to depend on the initial endowment of securities $\hat{\mathbf{x}}^i$. This dependence is surprising since intuitively one expects the final portfolio and its properties to be independent of the initial portfolio. This apparent anomaly is solved as follows. The presence of the wealth constraint means that the choice of the final portfolio is limited in size but not in composition by an individual's initial endowment. The apparent dependence on the initial endowment $\hat{\mathbf{x}}^i$ can be reduced to a dependence on only the magnitude of the initial wealth. This fact is established in Corollary 5.3.1.

COROLLARY 5.3.1.

$$\frac{d\psi^i}{dW^i} = \frac{\sum\limits_{j=1}^{n} \psi^i_j(x^i_j - \hat{x}^i_j)}{\sum\limits_{j=1}^{n} \mu^i_j(x^i_j - \hat{x}^i_j)} \Rightarrow \frac{d\psi^i}{dW^i} = \frac{\sum\limits_{j=1}^{n} \psi^i_j x^i_j - (\psi^i_n/p_n)V^i_0}{W^i - (1 + r^i_n)V^i_0}.$$

PROOF. Let an individual trade his initial endowment $\hat{\mathbf{x}}^i = (\hat{x}^i_1, \dots, \hat{x}^i_n)$ for an endowment in only one security, say the $n$th. Then we have

$$\hat{x}^i_j = 0 \qquad j \neq n \qquad \hat{x}^i_n = \frac{V^i_0}{p_n}$$

$$\therefore \quad \frac{d\psi^i}{dW^i} = \frac{\sum\limits_{j=1}^{n} \psi^i_j(x^i_j - \hat{x}^i_j)}{\sum\limits_{j=1}^{n} \mu^i_j(x^i_j - \hat{x}^i_j)} = \frac{\sum\limits_{j=1}^{n} \psi^i_j x^i_j - (\psi^i_n V^i_0)/(p_n)}{\sum\limits_{j=1}^{n} \mu^i_j x^i_j - (\mu^i_n/p_n)V^i_0}$$

$$= \frac{\sum\limits_{j=1}^{n} \psi^i_j x^i_j - (\psi^i_n/p_n)V^i_0}{W^i - (1 + r^i_n)V^i_0}$$

Q.E.D.

The device of giving an individual his entire endowment in only one security is seen to be equivalent to the choice of a reference security. *This corollary establishes that there is an irreducible dependence on the initial endowment only with respect to the magnitude of initial wealth and not with respect to the details of the composition of the endowment.* This dependence arises from the necessity of expressing results in terms of a reference security or a reference level of risk and return.

## 5.5. The Market-Equilibrium Solution

In Chapter 4 we showed that the number of equilibrium equations (the first-order conditions for personal equilibrium, the wealth constraint, and the market-clearing conditions) is equal to the number of variables when one equation is omitted to account for redundancy.[7] In this section we shall outline a general procedure for obtaining the equilibrium solution in the general two-parameter functional representation. This solution will be a specification of the values of the variables at market equilibrium. Since the exact values depend on the form of the function $f^i(W^i, \psi^i)$, only an indication of the procedure for obtaining a solution can be given without explicitly specifying the form of $f(W, \psi)$ for each individual.

[7] See Tables 4.1 and 4.2.

In the following analysis we assume a solution exists, state the solution procedure, then discuss properties of the solution and, finally, present a flow diagram for a solution algorithm.

**5.5.1. Solution Procedure.** When $\lambda^i$ is eliminated from the first-order conditions and security $n$ is used as a reference security, we have

$$f^i_1(\mu^i_j - \mu^i_n q_j) + f^i_2(\psi^i_j - \psi^i_n q_j) = 0 \qquad j = 1, \ldots, n - 1$$

$$\sum_{j=1}^{n} q_j(x^i_j - \hat{x}^i_j) = 0.$$

When the $\mathbf{q}_j = (q_1, \ldots, q_{n-1})$ is regarded as a parameter by individual $i$, we have $n$ equations in $n$ unknowns, the portfolio position of individual $i$. When these equations of personal equilibrium are solved, they specify the amount individual $i$ will buy of each security, given his expectations, utility function, and initial endowment as a function of relative prices. This solution is denoted symbolically as

$$x^i_j = x^i_j(\mathbf{q}|\hat{\mathbf{x}}^i, \tilde{\boldsymbol{\mu}}^i) \qquad j = 1, \ldots, n, \tag{5.25}$$

where | after $\mathbf{q}$ indicates the parameters upon which the solution is dependent, and the tilde over the vector of future prices makes explicit the fact that the solution is dependent on the expectations of individual $i$. The dependence on the form of $f^i(W^i, \psi^i)$ has not been indicated in Solution 5.25.

Equation 5.25 describes personal equilibrium. To obtain the relative prices that will clear markets, impose the market clearing condition,

$$\sum_{i=1}^{m} x^i_j(\mathbf{q}|\hat{\mathbf{x}}^i, \boldsymbol{\mu}^i) = X_j \qquad j = 1, \ldots, n - 1, \tag{5.26}$$

where $X_j$, the total number of shares outstanding, is a given parameter.

The market-clearing condition has been imposed upon only $(n - 1)$ of the securities, since one of the market-clearing equations is redundant. As a matter of convenience the $n$th equation has been chosen as the redundant equation.

Equation 5.26 is a set of $n - 1$ *independent* equations in the $n - 1$ relative prices. Assuming that the solution exists, these equations will yield the values of relative prices that will clear all markets in terms of given parameters, i.e., each individual's initial endowment of securities, the total number of outstanding shares of each security, and the parameters of each individual's expectations.

NOTATION. Let $\mathbf{q}^* = (q^*_1, \ldots, q^*_{n-1})$ be the *optimal relative price vector*, i.e., the vector of relative prices that clears all markets and thereby provides market equilibrium.

To obtain the position of each individual in each security, substitute $\mathbf{q}^*$ into Equation 5.25 to obtain the personal equilibrium values corresponding to equilibrium prices, i.e.,

$$x_j^i = x_j^i(\mathbf{q}^*|\hat{\mathbf{x}}^i, \tilde{\boldsymbol{\mu}}^i). \tag{5.27}$$

To summarize, the solution involves the following steps: (1) Solve for the equations of personal equilibrium for each individual to obtain

$$x_j^i = x_j^i(\mathbf{q}|\hat{\mathbf{x}}^i, \tilde{\boldsymbol{\mu}}^i) \qquad j = 1, \ldots, n.$$

(2) Impose the market-clearing requirement,

$$\sum_{i=1}^m x_j^i(\mathbf{q}|\hat{\mathbf{x}}^i, \tilde{\boldsymbol{\mu}}^i) = X_j,$$

to obtain $n - 1$ equations in the $n - 1$ relative prices giving $\mathbf{q}^* = (q_1^*, \ldots, q_{n-1}^*)$. (3) Substitute $\mathbf{q}^*$ into Equation 5.25 to obtain $x_j^i$ at market equilibrium for every $i$ and $j$.

**5.5.2. Characteristics of the Equilibrium Solution.** The following observations are relevant.

1. There is considerable structure in the system of equations. Each individual's personal-equilibrium equations are linked to each other individual's personal-equilibrium equations only through (relative) prices. They do not depend explicitly on the position variables of other individuals.

2. Since $\mathbf{q}^*$ depends on both $\mathbf{X} = (X_1, \ldots, X_{n-1})$ and the initial endowment $\hat{\mathbf{x}}^i$ of each individual, the position of individual $i$ in security $j$ depends on not only his own endowment of securities, but also on the endowment of all other individuals and the total outstanding stock of all other securities. The role of the initial endowment is to determine the total wealth available for an individual with a particular utility function and set of expectations.

3. Since $x_j^i = x_j^i(\mathbf{q}|\hat{\mathbf{x}}^i, \tilde{\boldsymbol{\mu}}^i)$ depends on the form of individual $i$'s utility function, and since $\mathbf{q}^*$ is obtained from the market-clearing conditions, $\mathbf{q}^*$ depends on the form of the utility function of each individual. This dependence, which is hidden in $x_j^i(\mathbf{q}|\hat{\mathbf{x}}^i, \tilde{\boldsymbol{\mu}}^i)$ in Equation 5.26, is usually a source of considerable complexity.

4. Since $x_j^i = x_j^i(\mathbf{q}^*|\hat{\mathbf{x}}^i, \tilde{\boldsymbol{\mu}}^i)$ is the equilibrium value of $x_j^i$, this value depends not only on the form of individual $i$'s own utility function, but through its dependence on relative prices, on the form of each individual's utility function. Thus, *although it has been assumed that the expected utility function of an individual depends only on the portfolio position of the individual, the actual equilibrium position depends on the utility function of all individuals in the market.*

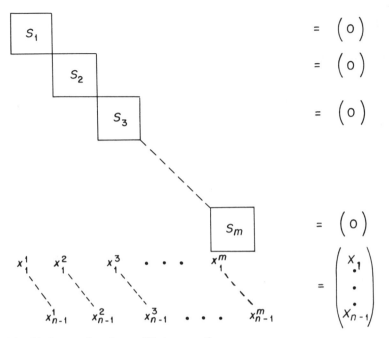

Fig. 5.1. System of market-equilibrium equations.

## 5.6. A Solution Algorithm

The system of market-equilibrium equations has considerable structure. It can be represented in an almost block diagonal form, as shown in Figure 5.1, where $S^i$ is the system of personal equilibrium equations defined by Equations 5.2 and 5.3. The linkage between the personal equilibrium equations is given by the market clearing requirements.

This structure and the solution procedure outlined suggest a computerized solution procedure which is a sort of algorithmic *tatonnement*. Given the parameters of the problem, it is to

(1) choose a starting set of relative prices;
(2) solve equations of personal equilibrium for each individual;
(3) test for market clearing;
(4) print the present solution and stop if all markets are cleared;
(5) adjust prices if all markets are not cleared;
(6) go to Step 2.

This very rough algorithm is diagramed in Figure 5.2. The key to the success of such an algorithm is a good price-adjustment rule as well as an efficient solution algorithm for a set of nonlinear equations describing

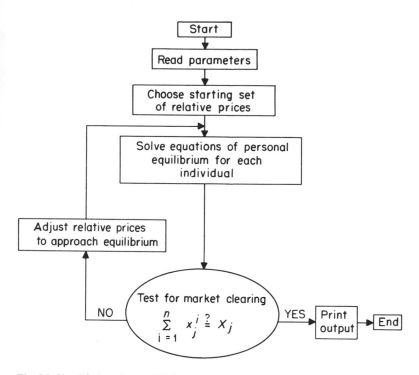

Fig. 5.2. Simplified market-equilibrium solution procedure.

personal equilibrium. Note that if there are multiple maxima for any individual's personal equilibrium problem, this algorithm does not guarantee a unique optimal solution to the market equilibrium problem.

### 5.7. The Case of a Riskless Asset

DEFINITION 5.4. An asset $k$ will be *riskless to the* $i$th *individual* if and only if $\partial \psi^i / \partial x_k^i = 0$ for all values of $x_k^i$.

DEFINITION 5.5. An asset $k$ will be *universally riskless* if and only if $\partial \psi^i / \partial x_k^i = 0$ for all values $x_k^i$ and for every individual.

When the $n$th asset is riskless, the first-order conditions for personal equilibrium given by Equation 5.4 become

$$f_1^i \mu_j^i + f_2^i \psi_j^i = \lambda^i p_j \qquad j = 1, \dots, n-1 \tag{5.28}$$

$$f_1^i \mu_n^i = \lambda^i p_n. \tag{5.29}$$

The presence of the riskless asset means that $\lambda^i$ can be expressed as

$$\lambda^i = f_1^i \frac{\mu_n^i}{p_n}. \tag{5.30}$$

Unlike the expression for $\lambda^i$ given by Equation 5.7 for the general case, $\lambda^i$ does not depend on the marginal risk of the reference security.

THEOREM 5.4. When asset $n$ is riskless to individual $i$, the rate of substitution of risk for return is given by

$$\frac{d\psi^i}{dW^i} = \frac{\psi_j^i}{p_j[(\mu_j^i/p_j) - (\mu_n^i/p_n)]} = \frac{\psi_j^i}{p_j(r_j^i - r_n^i)}. \tag{5.31}$$

PROOF. From Equation 5.6 we have

$$\frac{d\psi^i}{dW^i} = \frac{\psi_j^i - (p_j/p_n)\psi_n^i}{\mu_j^i - \mu_n^i(p_j/p_n)}.$$

Since $\psi_n^i = 0$ when asset $n$ is riskless to $i$, this becomes

$$\frac{d\psi^i}{dW^i} = \frac{\psi_j^i}{\mu_j^i - \mu_n^i(p_j/p_n)} = \frac{\psi_j^i}{p_j[(\mu_j^i/p_j) - (\mu_n^i/p_n)]} = \frac{\psi_j^i}{p_j(r_j^i - r_n^i)}.$$

Q.E.D.

Theorem 5.4 asserts that when asset $n$ is riskless for individual $i$, then the rate of substitution of risk for return is equal to the ratio of the marginal risk of asset $j$ to the expected dollar return for risk-bearing. The interpretation of $p_j(r_j^i - r_n^i)$ as the expected dollar return for risk-bearing is based on the following argument: The quantity $r_n^i$ is the rate of return per dollar for waiting. It is in effect a pure interest rate. The difference between the return on asset $j$ and the riskless asset $n$ is then a return for risk-bearing.[8] Then $p_j$ times $(r_j - r_n)$ is the dollar return per share for risk-bearing.

Note that the numerator of Equation 5.31 contains only a marginal risk and not a relative marginal risk. The presence of a riskless asset has made it possible to eliminate the need for a reference security from which risk is measured. The reference level may now be regarded as zero, and the measure of risk absolute rather than relative. This situation is another reason for regarding marginal portfolio risk as the measure of risk for an individual security.

COROLLARY 5.4.1. When asset $n$ is riskless to individual $i$, the ratio of marginal risk to dollar compensation for risk-bearing for individual $i$ is the same for

---

[8] That $r_j^i - r_n^i$ be negative is not precluded and, in fact, is possible.

every security, i.e.,

$$\frac{\psi_j^i}{p_j(r_j^i - r_n^i)} = \frac{\psi_k^i}{p_k(r_k^i - r_n^i)} \qquad j, k = 1, \ldots, n - 1. \tag{5.32}$$

PROOF. Equation 5.32 follows immediately from Equation 5.31 since the left-hand side of 5.31 is independent of the subscript.

COROLLARY 5.4.2. When asset $n$ is riskless, the ratio of marginal risk per dollar to risk premium is the same for every security, i.e.,

$$\frac{\Psi_j^i}{m_j^i} = \frac{\Psi_k^i}{m_k^i} \qquad j, k = 1, \ldots, n - 1. \tag{5.33}$$

PROOF. Equation 5.32 can be rewritten as

$$\frac{\psi_j^i/p_j}{r_j^i - r_n^i} = \frac{\psi_k^i/p_k}{r_k^i - r_n^i} \qquad \text{for every } j, k = 1, \ldots, n - 1$$

$$\Rightarrow \frac{\Psi_j^i}{m_j^i} = \frac{\Psi_k^i}{m_k^i} \quad \text{since } \Psi_j^i \equiv \frac{\psi_j^i}{p_j} \quad \text{and} \quad m_j^i \equiv r_j^i - r_n^i.$$

Q.E.D.

THEOREM 5.5. When asset $n$ is riskless to individual $i$, the rate of substitution of risk for return can be expressed as

$$\frac{d\Psi^i}{d\rho^i} = \frac{\sum\limits_{j=1}^{n} \Psi_j^i y_j^i}{\rho^i - r_n^i} \tag{5.34}$$

and

$$\frac{d\psi^i}{dW^i} = \frac{\sum\limits_{j=1}^{n-1} \psi_j^i x_j^i}{W^i - (1 + r_n^i)V_0^i}. \tag{5.35}$$

PROOF. When asset $n$ is riskless, $\psi_n^i = \Psi_n^i = 0$. Setting $\psi_n^i = 0$ and $\Psi_n^i = 0$ in Equations 5.21 and 5.22 gives Equations 5.34 and 5.35, respectively.

Q.E.D.

Note that the role of the riskless asset has been to eliminate $\psi_n^i$ or $\Psi_n^i$ from the general equations. We can again regard the riskless asset as specifying zero as the reference level for risk; it therefore makes the measure of risk absolute rather than relative and simplifies the nature of the equations describing personal equilibrium. We shall see that this simplification is a critical part of the ability to solve for a closed-form relation between portfolio risk and portfolio return.

The proofs of Theorems 5.4 and 5.5 have been straightforward, easy derivations because they have involved specializing the general results of Theorems 5.1 and 5.2 and their corollaries. The facility with which these results were obtained is indicative of the power and clarity of a general formulation.

Although the proofs of Theorems 5.4 and 5.5 have been obtained with ease, insight into the way in which the existence of a riskless asset simplified the problem can be obtained by a brute-force proof patterned on the general proofs. These proofs will not, however, be provided in this book.

### 5.8. Homogeneous Risk Measures

In this section we shall establish that homogeneity of the risk function with respect to the security position will lead to important simplifications in the previous results, especially for the case of a riskless asset. Previous work, even in the context of specialized models, has not recognized the critical role played by homogeneity of the risk function.

The class of homogeneous risk measures contains both variance and standard deviation. Other homogeneous measures of risk include the class of loss functions $L = \int_{-\infty}^{a} (\tilde{W} - \overline{W})^k dF(\tilde{W})$ which are homogeneous of degree $k$. Semivariance is a special case of this general loss function in which $a = \overline{W}$ and $k = 2$. It will be shown that many of the nice properties of standard deviation and variance arise from their homogeneity including the ability to specify closed-form relations for the locus of possible risk-return combinations.

DEFINITION 5.6. A function $g(x_1, x_2, \ldots, x_n)$ is said to be *homogeneous* of degree $k$ if and only if

$$g(cx_1, cx_2, \ldots, cx_n) = c^k g(x_1, x_2, \ldots, x_n)$$

for every constant $c \neq 0$.

NOTATION. Let $H^k$ be the class of functions that are homogeneous of degree $k$. Then $g(x_1, x_2, \ldots, x_n) \in H^k$ will be read "$g$ belongs to the class of functions that are homogeneous of degree $k$."

A result from the calculus of homogeneous functions will be worked overtime in this book. It is known as Euler's theorem and is stated here for future reference.

EULER'S THEOREM. A function $g(x_1, \ldots, x_n) \in H^k$ over a region $\Leftrightarrow$

$$\sum_{i=1}^{n} \frac{dg}{dx_i} x_i = kg(x_1, \ldots, x_n).$$

This equation is frequently called *Euler's formula*.

We are now in a position to state and prove an important theorem.

THEOREM 5.6. If asset $n$ is riskless to individual $i$ and if $\psi^i(x^i_1, \ldots, x^i_{n-1}) \in H^k$, then

$$\frac{d\psi^i}{dW^i} = \frac{k\psi^i}{W^i - (1 + r^i_n)V^i_0}. \tag{5.36}$$

PROOF. If $\psi^i(x^i_1, \ldots, x^i_{n-1}) \in H^k$, then by Euler's theorem

$$\sum_{j=1}^{n-1} \psi^i_j x^i_j = \sum_{j=1}^{n-1} \frac{\partial \psi^i}{\partial x^i_j} x^i_j = k\psi^i.$$

Therefore, Expression 5.35 for $d\psi^i/dW^i$ when asset $n$ is riskless to $i$ becomes

$$\frac{d\psi^i}{dW^i} = \frac{\sum\limits_{j=1}^{n-1} \psi^i_j x^i_j}{W^i - (1 + r^i_n)V^i_0} = \frac{k\psi^i}{W^i - (1 + r^i_n)V^i_0}.$$

Q.E.D.

COROLLARY 5.6.1. If asset $n$ is riskless to individual $i$ and $\psi^i \in H^k$, then

$$\frac{d\Psi^i}{d\rho^i} = \frac{k\Psi^i}{\rho^i - r^i_n}. \tag{5.37}$$

PROOF. From Theorem 5.6,

$$\frac{d\psi^i}{dW^i} = \frac{k\psi^i}{W^i - (1 + r^i_n)V^i_0} = \frac{k(\psi^i/V^i_0)}{(W^i - V^i_0)/(V^i_0) - r^i_n} = \frac{k\Psi^i}{\rho^i - r^i_n}$$

$$\Rightarrow \frac{d\Psi^i}{d\rho^i} = \frac{k\Psi^i}{\rho^i - r^i_n}$$

since by Lemma 5.3, $\quad \dfrac{d\psi^i}{dW^i} = \dfrac{d\Psi^i}{d\rho^i}.$

Q.E.D.

## 5.9. Risk-Return Relationships

We shall now investigate risk-return relationships for the two-parameter functional representation. We initiate the analysis with a discussion of terms and solution methods.

DEFINITION 5.7. An *efficient locus* is the set of risk-return points consistent with the wealth constraint and the solution of the $n - 1$ equations:

$$\frac{d\psi}{d\overline{W}} = \frac{\psi_j - \psi_n q_j}{\mu_j - \mu_n q_j} \qquad j = 1, \ldots, n - 1 \tag{5.38}$$

or

$$\frac{d\Psi}{d\rho} = \frac{\Psi_j - \Psi_n}{r_j - r_n} \qquad j = 1, \ldots, n - 1. \tag{5.39}$$

The efficient locus is a set of risk-return combinations arising from equations that are a subset of the first-order conditions for maximizing expected utility subject to a wealth constraint. The reader should contrast this concept with the idea of the efficient frontier, which summarizes risk-return relations that minimize risk for any given level of return.

When asset $n$ is riskless and $\Psi \in H^k$, it can be shown that the efficient locus in the $(\rho, \Psi)$ plane will be defined by the solution to $d\Psi/d\rho = k\Psi/(\rho - r_n)$ by showing (1) that this equation arises from Equation 5.39 and the wealth constraint (cf. Corollary 5.6.1); and (2) by showing that the solution to this differential equation (which is given by Equation 5.42) is consistent with Equation 5.39. A comparable statement can be made for the $(W, \psi)$ locus.

The efficient locus has been defined to discuss risk-return relationships. It will summarize the risk-return properties that do not depend on the explicit form of the function in the TPFR but do depend on the investor's risk measure and his expectations. It is a summary measure in that it deals with risk-return properties rather than portfolios per se. The optimal risk-return position that maximizes expected utility will lie on the efficient locus.

**5.9.1. Efficient Loci.** THEOREM 5.7. If asset $n$ is riskless to individual $i$ and if $\psi^i \in H^k$, then individual $i$'s efficient locus in the $(W, \psi)$ plane is given by

$$\psi^i = b^i[W^i - (1 + r_n^i)V_0^i]^k \tag{5.40}$$

or

$$W^i - (1 + r_n^i)V_0^i = a^i \sqrt[k]{\psi^i} \tag{5.41}$$

where $a^i$ and $b^i$ are constants characteristic of individual $i$ when prices are fixed.

PROOF. When asset $n$ is riskless to individual $i$ and $\psi^i \in H^k$, then Equation 5.36 gives

$$\frac{d\psi^i}{dW^i} = \frac{k\psi^i}{W^i - (1 + r_n^i)V_0^i}$$

$$\Rightarrow \frac{d\psi^i}{\psi^i} = \frac{k\,dW^i}{W^i - (1 + r_n^i)V_0^i}$$

$$\Rightarrow \psi^i = b^i[W^i - (1 + r_n^i)V_0^i]^k$$

$$\Rightarrow W^i - (1 + r_n^i)V_0^i = a^i \sqrt[k]{\psi^i} \quad \text{where } b^i = (a^i)^{-k}.$$

Q.E.D.

In general $a^i$ and $b^i$ will be functions of prices.

COROLLARY 5.7.1. If asset $n$ is riskless to individual $i$ and if $\psi^i \in H^k$, then the efficient locus in the $(\rho, \Psi)$ plane is described by

$$\Psi^i = \beta^i(\rho^i - r_n^i)^k \tag{5.42}$$

or

$$(\rho^i - r_n^i) = \alpha^i \sqrt[k]{\Psi^i} \tag{5.43}$$

where $\alpha^i$ and $\beta^i$ are constants characteristic of individual $i$.

Two proofs of this result will be given. The first proof will be based on a change of variables from $(W^i, \psi^i)$ to $(\rho^i, \Psi^i)$. It will establish the relationship between constants in the two formulations of the efficient frontier. The second is a direct proof based on the expression for the rate of substitution which shows that the $(\rho^i, \Psi^i)$ efficient locus is also the solution of a differential equation.

PROOF 1. Dividing Equation 5.41 by $V_0^i$ and rewriting this expression gives

$$\frac{W^i - V_0^i}{V_0^i} - r_n^i = \frac{a^i \sqrt[k]{V_0^i}}{V_0^i} \sqrt[k]{\frac{\psi^i}{V_0^i}}$$

$$\Rightarrow \rho^i - r_n^i = \alpha^i \sqrt[k]{\Psi^i} \quad \text{where } \alpha^i = a^i(V_0^i)^{(1/k)-1}$$

$$\Rightarrow \Psi^i = \beta^i(\rho^i - r_n^i)^k \quad \text{where } \beta^i = (\alpha^i)^{-k}.$$

Q.E.D.

PROOF 2. From Corollary 5.6.1 we have, when $\psi^i \in H^k$ and asset $n$ is riskless to individual $i$,

$$\left(\frac{d\Psi^i}{d\rho}\right)_{\mathbf{p}} = \frac{k\Psi^i}{\rho^i - r_n^i}$$

$$\frac{(d\Psi^i)_{\mathbf{p}}}{\Psi^i} = \frac{k(d\rho^i)_{\mathbf{p}}}{\rho^i - r_n^i},$$

where the subscript on the differential emphasizes that prices are held constant. By integrating the preceding expression and simplifying, one obtains

$$ln(\Psi^i) = kln(\rho^i - r_n^i) + const$$

$$\Rightarrow \Psi^i = \beta^i(\rho^i - r_n^i)^k$$

$$\Rightarrow (\rho^i - r_n^i) = \alpha^i \sqrt[k]{\Psi^i} \tag{5.44}$$

where $\beta^i = (\alpha^i)^{-k}$ are constants of integration for fixed prices, but which will in general be functions of prices.[9]

Q.E.D.

It is emphasized that the efficient risk-return loci derived above are personal equilibrium relationships derived for a fixed set of prices. The constants $a^i$ and $b^i$ (or $\alpha^i$ and $\beta^i$) are really functions of prices; as prices change the "constants of integration" will change and the position of the efficient locus in the risk-return plane will shift.

**5.9.2. Interpretation of Homogeneity—Returns to Scale.** A homogeneous function has the following scaling property: If all variables are scaled by the same factor $c$, then the function will be scaled by $c^k$ if the function is homogeneous of degree $k$. (This property is true by definition of a homogeneous function.)

Two interpretations can be placed on a homogeneous risk function. These are in terms of what an individual either expects or demands to receive when he changes the scale of his investment. For instance, if $k > 1$, then it can be said that the individual either expects or demands decreasing returns to risk-bearing. When $k = 1$, the individual either expects or demands constant returns to the scale of risk-bearing. Thus the value of $k$ indicates whether there is increasing, constant, or decreasing returns to risk-bearing according to whether $k < 1$, $k = 1$, or $k > 1$ respectively. These cases are sketched in Figures 5.3 and 5.4 in both the wealth-risk and the return-risk planes. These figures show that the efficient locus is linear only when $k = 1$. However, a plot of the $\sqrt[k]{\psi^i}$ versus $W^i$ or $\sqrt[k]{\Psi^i}$ versus $\rho^i$ is always linear, as shown in the graphs of Figures 5.5 and 5.6.

Observe that efficient combinations of wealth and risk will usually have different intercepts for different individuals since they will have different initial endowments of wealth $V_0^i$ as well as different expected returns for holding the riskless asset. However, differences in the intercept for the plot of $\sqrt[k]{\Psi^i}$ versus $\rho^i$ will arise only because of differences among individuals in the expected return on the riskless asset.

**5.9.3. Homogeneity and Scaling.** In the preceding analysis we have derived a number of expressions for the efficient locus and related equations and interpreted homogeneity in terms of returns to scale. Theorem 5.8 establishes conditions under which the efficient locus can be generated by scaling the investment in the portfolio of risky assets.

THEOREM 5.8. If asset $n$ is riskless to individual $i$ and if $\psi^i \in H^k$, then the efficient locus can be generated by scaling the investment in risky assets.

---

[9] In Chapter 7 explicit solutions for the constant as a function of prices is given in Theorem 7.3 and Corollary 7.3.1.

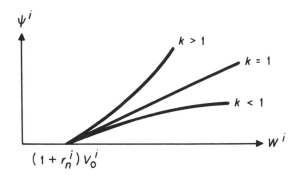

Fig. 5.3. $(W^i, \Psi^i)$ efficient locus for $\psi^i \in H^k$.

To prove Theorem 5.8, it is sufficient to show (1) that the equations defining the efficient locus are independent of the scale of investment in risky assets; and (2) that the level of investment in risky assets can be scaled without violating the wealth constraint.

PROOF. 1. Let $w = \sum_{j=1}^{n-1} y_j$ be the relative investment in risky assets and $y_n = 1 - w$ be the investment in the riskless asset. Define $h_j = y_j/w$ as the relative investment in riskless asset $j$ where $\sum_{j=1}^{n-1} h_j = 1$.

2. We now show that the equation $\Psi = \alpha(\rho - r_n)^k$ and the equations defining the efficient locus are independent of the value of $w$. The risk $\Psi$ is independent of $y_n$ since asset $n$ is riskless. Therefore,

$$\Psi(y_1, \ldots, y_{n-1}) = \Psi(wh_1, \ldots, wh_{n-1}) = w^k \Psi(h_1, \ldots, h_{n-1}) \qquad (5.45)$$

$$\rho - r_n = \sum_{j=1}^{n} (r_j - r_n)y_j \quad \text{since } \sum_{j=1}^{n} y_j = 1$$

$$\therefore \quad \rho - r_n = w \sum_{j=1}^{n-1} (r_j - r_n)h_j = w(r - r_n) \quad \text{where } r \equiv \sum_{j=1}^{n-1} r_j h_j. \qquad (5.46)$$

Using these expressions, we show that Equation 5.42 is independent of $w$ as follows:

$$\Psi(y_1, \ldots, y_n) = \beta(\rho - r_n)^k$$

$$\Leftrightarrow \Psi(wh_1, \ldots, wh_{n-1}) = \beta[w(r - r_n)]^k$$

$$\Leftrightarrow w^k \Psi(h) = \beta w^k \left[ \sum_{j=1}^{n-1} (r_j - r_n)h_j \right]^k$$

$$\Leftrightarrow \Psi(h) = \beta \left[ \sum_{j=1}^{n-1} (r_j - r_n)h_j \right]^k. \qquad (5.47)$$

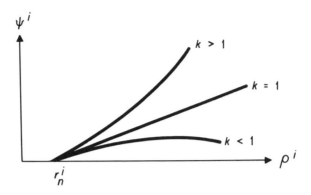

Fig. 5.4. $(\rho^i, \psi^i)$ efficient locus for $\psi^i \in H^k$.

Equation 5.42 is clearly independent of $w$, which is what is to be shown.

To show that the other first-order equations are also independent of $w$, consider

$$\frac{\Psi_j}{r_j - r_n} = \frac{d\Psi}{d\rho} = \frac{k\Psi}{\rho - r_n}. \tag{5.48}$$

Since both $\Psi_j$ and $\Psi/(\rho - r_n) \in H^{k-1}$, Equation 5.48 is also independent of $w$.
3. Finally, to show that scaling is possible, let the following variable transformation be defined:

$$y_j^+ = (1 + \Delta)y_j \qquad j = 1, \ldots, n - 1 \tag{5.49}$$

$$y_n^+ = -\Delta \sum_{j=1}^{n-1} y_j + y_n. \tag{5.50}$$

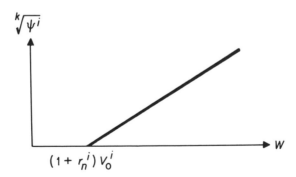

Fig. 5.5. The $k^{th}$ root of $\psi^i$ vs. $W^i$.

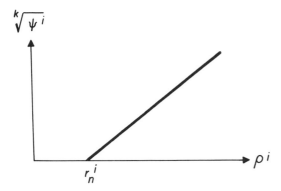

Fig. 5.6. The $k^{th}$ root of $\Psi^i$ vs. $\rho^i$.

Clearly, $\sum_{j=1}^{n-1} y_j^+ = 1$ if $\sum_{j=1}^{n} y_j = 1$. Moreover, $w$ is scaled by $1 + \Delta$ since

$$w^+ = \sum_{j=1}^{n-1} y_j^+ = (1 + \Delta) \sum_{j=1}^{n-1} y_j = (1 + \Delta)w.$$

Hence, the transformation defined by Equations 5.49 and 5.50 scales the investment in risky assets and satisfies the wealth constraint. Thus, if $(y_1, \ldots, y_n)$ is a solution, Equations 5.49 and 5.50 will generate other solutions as $\Delta$ is varied. These will develop the curve that is the efficient locus.

Q.E.D.

Note that extensive use has been made of both the facts that asset $n$ is riskless and that $\Psi \in H^k$. Both are crucial for the proof.

The fact that Equation 5.47 is independent of the scale of investment in the riskless asset when $\psi \in H^k$ does not mean that the optimal solution is independent of the value of $w$. However, the determination of $w$ requires explicit consideration of the form of the function defining how expected utility depends on risk and return. Thus, explicit reference must be made to the utility function; such reference has not occurred in deriving the efficient locus. This analysis is continued in Chapter 7 for the special case of mean-variance models.

# 6

## Asset Selection with $\phi$ and $\pi$ as Risk Measures

In this chapter we very briefly indicate how the TPFR can be specialized to the risk measures $\phi$ and $\pi$, and we shall investigate one example. We shall refer to expected future wealth as $W$ without a bar over it; when we refer to the random variable, we will write $\tilde{W}$. Superscripts referring to individuals will be dropped since we shall confine our analysis to personal equilibrium relationships.

### 6.1. The Risk Measure $\phi$

THEOREM 6.1. The difference in security risk per dollar for any two securities is the marginal utility of wealth times the difference in return, i.e.,

$$\Phi_j - \Phi_n = U^{(1)}(W)(r_j - r_n). \tag{6.1}$$

PROOF. Form the Lagrangian for the objective function $\overline{U} = U(W) - \phi$

$$L = U(W) - \phi - \lambda\left(\sum_{j=1}^{n} p_j(x_j - \hat{x}_j)\right). \tag{6.2}$$

First-order conditions (excluding the wealth constraint) are

$$U^{(1)}(W)\mu_j - \phi_j - \lambda p_j = 0 \qquad j = 1,\ldots,n. \tag{6.3}$$

Eliminating $\lambda$ by using the $n$th equation and simplifying gives

$$U^{(1)}(W)\mu_j - \phi_j = U^{(1)}(W)(\mu_n q_j) - \phi_n q_j \quad \text{where } q_j = p_j/p_n$$

$$\Rightarrow \phi_j - \phi_n q_j = U^{(1)}(W)(\mu_j - \mu_n q_j) \tag{6.4}$$

$$\Rightarrow \frac{\phi_j}{p_j} - \frac{\phi_n}{p_n} = U^{(1)}(W)\left(\frac{\mu_j}{p_j} - \frac{\mu_n}{p_n}\right) \tag{6.5}$$

$$\Rightarrow \Phi_j - \Phi_n = U^{(1)}(W)(r_j - r_n). $$

Q.E.D.

The equation has the general structure,

$\Delta$ (security risk) = (marginal utility of wealth) $\cdot$ $\Delta$ (return).

COROLLARY 6.1.1. The rate of substitution of return for risk is given by the marginal utility of wealth evaluated at the distribution mean, i.e.,

$$\frac{d\Phi}{d\rho} = \frac{d\phi}{dW} = U^{(1)}(W). \tag{6.6}$$

PROOF. Rewriting Equation 6.1 as

$$r_j - r_n = \frac{1}{U^{(1)}(W)}(\Phi_j - \Phi_n), \tag{6.7}$$

and comparing this expression with Equation 5.22 for the TPFR, which is

$$r_j - r_n = \frac{d\rho}{d\Psi}(\Psi_j - \Psi_n),$$

reveals that

$$\frac{d\Phi}{d\rho} = U^{(1)}(W) = \frac{d\phi}{dW},$$

since $d\Phi/d\rho = d\phi/dW$ by Lemma 5.3.

Q.E.D.

This theorem could also have been proved by using Equation 6.2 to derive the differential $d\phi$. However, the proof given establishes the key link in transforming the results of Chapter 5 on the TPFR into the case for which $\phi$ is used as the risk measure. The rule is to replace the rate of substitution of risk for return with the marginal utility of wealth in all equations and substitute $\phi$ for $\psi$, then all equations for the TPFR are correct for the risk measure $\phi$.

Table 6.1 summarizes some of the major personal equilibrium equations of the TPFR when specialized to the GMC. Equivalent equations can be stated in terms of $\phi$ and $W$ as well as $\Phi$ and $\rho$.

**6.1.1. An Example of the Risk Measure $\phi$.** Let $U(\tilde{W}) = -e^{-c\tilde{W}}$, and let $\tilde{W}$ be normally distributed with a mean $W$ and a variance $V$. Since $W$ is normally distributed, this is a special case in which the mean-variance criterion applies.

TABLE 6.1. EQUATIONS IN THE GMC

| Equation | Restrictions |
|---|---|
| $\Phi_j - \Phi_n = U^{(1)}(\overline{W})(r_j - r_n)$ | General (cf. Theorem 6.1, Equation 6.1) |
| $\sum\limits_{j=1}^{n} \Phi_j y_j - \Phi_n = U^{(1)}(\overline{W})(\rho - r_n)$ | General (Sum over Equation 6.1) |
| $\Phi_j = U^{(1)}(\overline{W})(r_j - r_n)$ | $\Phi_n = 0$ |
| $\sum\limits_{j=1}^{n} \Phi_j y_j = U^{(1)}(\overline{W})(\rho - r_n)$ | $\Phi_n = 0$ |
| $k\Phi = U^{(1)}(\overline{W})(\rho - r_n)$ | $\Phi_n = 0$ and $\Phi \in H^k$ |

Therefore, an analysis of this case will not only provide an example of the risk measure $\phi$, but will also provide a basis for comparison with the mean-variance models.

In the following we shall compute marginal risks and use Equation 5.19 to find an expression for both $r_j - r_n$ and the efficient locus.

We showed in Chapter 3, Equation 3.37, that $\phi$ is given by

$$\phi = e^{-cW}(e^{c^2V/2} - 1)$$

where variance $V$ has replaced $s^2$ in Equation 3.37. Assume asset $n$ has no variance associated with it. Then, $\phi_j$ and $\phi_n$ are given by

$$\phi_j = -c\mu_j\phi + e^{-cW}e^{c^2V/2}\left(\frac{c^2V_j}{2}\right) \quad \text{where } V_j = \frac{dV}{dx_j} \tag{6.8}$$

$$\phi_n = -c\mu_n\phi \quad \text{since } V_n = 0 \text{ by assumption.} \tag{6.9}$$

$$\therefore \quad \frac{\phi_j}{p_j} - \frac{\phi_n}{p_n} = -c(r_j - r_n)\phi + e^{-cW}e^{c^2V/2}(c^2/2)v_j \tag{6.10}$$

where $v_j \equiv V_j/p_j$ is marginal variance per dollar.

Substituting Equation 6.10 into Equation 6.1 and using $U^{(1)}(W) = +ce^{-cW}$ for marginal wealth, gives

$$-c(r_j - r_n)\phi + e^{-cW}e^{c^2V/2}(c^2/2)v_j = ce^{-cW}(r_j - r_n).$$

Combining terms involving $r_j - r_n$ and using the fact that $\phi + e^{-cW} = e^{-cW}e^{c^2V/2}$ gives

$$(c^2/2)v_je^{-cW}e^{c^2V/2} = c(r_j - r_n)(e^{-cW} + \phi)$$

$$\Rightarrow \frac{c}{2}v_j = r_j - r_n \tag{6.11}$$

$$\Rightarrow \frac{c}{2}\sum_{j=1}^{n} v_jy_j = \sum_{j=1}^{n} r_jy_j - r_n$$

$$\Rightarrow cv = \rho - r_n. \tag{6.12}$$

Equation 6.11 relates the security risk premium to marginal variance per dollar; Equation 6.12 gives a closed-form relation between variance and portfolio return. Both of these equations have the general structure expected from the mean-variance formulation of the TPFR; however, they are somewhat simpler in form because of the structure imposed by assuming a particular objective function.

We shall now use Equation 6.12 to find the efficient locus, $\phi$ vs. $\rho$. Transforming from variance per dollar to variance, Equation 6.12 becomes

$$cV = (\rho - r_n)V_0 \tag{6.13}$$

$$\therefore \quad \frac{c^2V}{2} = \frac{c(\rho - r_n)V_0}{2} = \frac{c}{2}(W - (1 + r_n)V_0).$$

$$\therefore \quad \phi = e^{-cW}(e^{c^2V/2} - 1) = e^{-cW}[e^{(c/2)(W - (1 + r_n)V_0)}]. \tag{6.14}$$

Thus we have the $(\phi, W)$ efficient locus. The expression is fairly complex. Observe, however, that the $W$-axis intercept is $(1 + r_n)V_0$, as predicted by the general theory, for the $(V, W)$ efficient locus.

We shall consider this same example again after considering $\pi$ as a measure of risk.

## 6.2. The Risk Premium $\pi$ as a Special Case of the TPFR

THEOREM 6.2. If the risk premium $\pi$ is used as the measure of risk, then the difference in security return is given by the difference in security risk, i.e.,

$$r_j - r_n = \frac{\pi_j}{p_j} - \frac{\pi_n}{p_n} \tag{6.15}$$

where $\pi_j/p_j = (1/p_j)(d\pi/dx_j)$ is the marginal risk per dollar, which has been identified as the measure of security risk.

PROOF. Form the Lagrangian for the objective function $\overline{U} = U(W - \pi)$ subject to a wealth constraint:

$$L = U(W - \pi) - \lambda \left[ \sum_{j=1}^{n} p_j(x_j - \hat{x}_j) \right]. \tag{6.16}$$

First-order conditions (excluding the wealth constraint) are

$$U^{(1)}(W - \pi)(\mu_j - \pi_j) - \lambda p_j = 0 \quad j = 1, \dots, n \tag{6.17}$$

$$\Rightarrow U^{(1)}(W - \pi)\left(\frac{\mu_j}{p_j} - \frac{\pi_j}{p_j}\right) = U^{(1)}(W - \pi)\left(\frac{\mu_n}{p_n} - \frac{\pi_n}{p_n}\right)$$

$$\Rightarrow \frac{\mu_j}{p_j} - \frac{\mu_n}{p_n} = \frac{\pi_j}{p_j} - \frac{\pi_n}{p_n}$$

$$\Rightarrow r_j - r_n = \frac{\pi_j}{p_j} - \frac{\pi_n}{p_n}. \tag{6.18}$$

Q.E.D.

COROLLARY 6.2.1. If $\pi$ is used as a risk measure, the rate of substitution of risk for return is constant and equal to 1.

PROOF. Identify $\pi_j/p_j$ with $\Psi_j$ in Equation 5.22 and compare the form of Equation 5.22 with Equation 6.15; it is seen that the rate of substitution is constant and equal to 1 as claimed.

COROLLARY 6.2.2. The difference between portfolio return and security return for any security is given by

$$\rho - r_n = \sum_{j=1}^{n} \left(\frac{\pi_j}{p_j}\right) y_j - \frac{\pi_n}{p_n} \tag{6.19}$$

where security $n$ has been chosen as a reference security.

PROOF. Multiplying Equation 6.15 by $y_j$ and summing over all $j$, and using

$$\sum_{j=1}^{n} y_j = 1 \text{ gives}$$

$$\sum_{j=1}^{n} r_j y_j - r_n = \sum_{j=1}^{n} \left(\frac{\pi_j}{p_j}\right) y_j - \left(\frac{\pi_n}{p_n}\right)$$

$$\Rightarrow \rho - r_n = \sum_{j=1}^{n} \left(\frac{\pi_j}{p_j}\right) y_j - \left(\frac{\pi_n}{p_n}\right).$$

Q.E.D.

**6.2.1. Ambiguity in the Term *Risk Premium*.** We have used the term *risk premium* in three different ways in Chapters 3, 5, and 6. They are the dollar risk premium, $\pi$, the portfolio return risk premium $\rho - r_n$, and the security risk premium, $r_j - r_n$, for security $j$. One may convert $(\rho - r_n)$ to dollar units by multiplying by the initial wealth $V_0$. Then, $(\rho - r_n)V_0$ is the dollar increase in return that an investor receives by accepting the risk inherent in the portfolio.

The reader should beware of the following spurious argument: This quantity $(1 + r_n)V_0$ is the amount that the decision-maker could have for certain; therefore, $\pi = \overline{W} - CE = \overline{W} - (1 + r_n)V_0 = (\rho - r_n)V_0$. *This equation is not valid.* The reason is that, although $(1 + r_n)V_0$ may be had for certain, it is *not* in general the certainty equivalent $CE$ because it is not the certain amount that the decision-maker is willing to trade for the portfolio and be indifferent between $(1 + r_n)V_0$ and the portfolio with a dollar return $(1 + \rho)V_0$ and an associated risk. *The fact is that the difference in return, either $\rho - r_n$ or $r_j - r_n$, and the risk premium $\pi$ are different concepts of risk premiums.* The proper relation between the two measures is really given by Equations 6.15 and 6.19.

COROLLARY 6.2.3. If asset $n$ is riskless, $\pi = (\rho - r_n)V_0$ if and only if $\pi \in H^1$.

PROOF. If asset $n$ is riskless, $\pi_n = 0$ and Equation 6.19 becomes

$$\rho - r_n = \sum_{j=1}^{n} \left(\frac{\pi_j}{p_j}\right) y_j.$$

Now $(\rho - r_n)V_0$ will equal $\pi$ if and only if

$$\pi = V_0 \sum_{j=1}^{n} \left(\frac{\pi_j}{p_j}\right) y_j = \sum_{j=1}^{n} \pi_j \left(\frac{y_j V_0}{p_j}\right) = \sum_{j=1}^{n} \pi_j x_j$$

and

$$\pi = \sum_{j=1}^{n} \pi_j x_j \Leftrightarrow \pi \in H^1.$$

Q.E.D.

**6.2.2. An Example of the Risk Measure $\pi$.** We shall now give an example of the risk measure $\pi$ for an exponential utility function under a normal distribution with asset $n$ riskless. We shall compute an expression for the security risk premium and the efficient locus. Let $U(\tilde{W}) = -e^{-c\tilde{W}}$. Under a normal distribution we showed $\pi = cV/2$ in Equation 3.38 where $V$, the variance of wealth, has replaced $s^2$ in Equation 3.38.

Transforming to risk per dollar gives

$$\frac{\pi}{V_0} = \frac{c}{2}\frac{V}{V_0} = \frac{c}{2}v$$

where $v = V/V_0 = \sum_{j=1}^{n-1}\sum_{k=1}^{n-1} \sigma_{jk} y_j y_k$ is variance per dollar. Therefore,

$$\frac{\pi_j}{p_j} = \frac{d}{dy_j}\left(\frac{\pi}{V_0}\right) = c\sum_{k=1}^{n-1} \sigma_{jk} y_k.$$

Substituting this expression for $\pi_j/p_j$ into Equations 6.15 and 6.19 and setting $\pi_n = 0$ gives

$$r_j - r_n = c\sum_{k=1}^{n-1} \sigma_{jk} y_k \tag{6.20}$$

$$\rho - r_n = c\sum_{j=1}^{n-1}\sum_{k=1}^{n-1} \sigma_{jk} y_j y_k = cv = 2\frac{\pi}{V_0}. \tag{6.21}$$

Equation 6.20 is similar in structure to the expression derived for $r_j - r_n$ for the mean-variance models. This similarity is expected, since $\pi$ is proportional to variance. Equation 6.21 is somewhat simpler since the rate of substitution of risk for return is unity and the expression on the right-hand side of Equation 6.20 is simply the marginal risk. It is, however, a sum of covariance terms.

Equation 6.21 describes the efficient locus in the $(\rho, \pi/V_0)$ plane. The locus is linear, with an intercept on the $\rho$-axis of $r_n$ and a slope of 2. This result does differ from the TPFR equation. For the TPFR, we have to solve the differential equation

$$\rho - r_n = \frac{d\rho}{dv}(2v)$$

to get the efficient locus. The fact that $d\rho/dv$ is known to be 1 has resulted in the simplification. The added structure involved in using a particular function, $U(W - \pi)$, to represent expected utility has greatly simplified the problem.

We now compare results using $\phi$ and $\pi$ as risk measures for $U(W) = -\exp(-cW)$ for $\tilde{W}$ normally distributed. When $v_j = 2\sum_k \sigma_{jk} y_k$ is substituted for $v_j$ in Equation 6.11, we see that the expressions for $r_j - r_n$ given by Equations 6.11 and 6.20 are the same. Moreover, Equations 6.12 and 6.21 for variance as a function of return are the same. The derivation of these expressions was considerably easier using $\pi$ as the risk measure than using $\phi$.

The efficient $(\rho, \phi)$ and $(\rho, \pi)$ loci are, however, not the same although one can be derived from the other if one knows the relation between $\phi$ and $\pi$. The distinction between the two efficient loci (other than functional form and complexity) is that the $(\rho, \phi)$ efficient locus depends on $\overline{W}$ and bends down; the $(\rho, \pi)$ efficient locus does not depend on $\overline{W}$ and is linear. Thus, we have a significant difference in the efficient loci using the two risk measures.

The fact that $\phi_n \neq 0$ when $\pi_n = 0$ in the examples is particularly interesting. It shows that one may or may not regard an asset as riskless depending on whether $\phi$ or $\pi$ is chosen as the risk measure. These observations suggest that the relations established between $\phi$ and $\pi$ in Theorem 3.2 are very weak criteria of comparability and that the two measures do have different implications, as for instance, whether or not asset $n$ is regarded as riskless.

Although this example has $\pi_n = 0$ and $\phi_n \neq 0$ when asset $n$ has zero variance, the converse relation is also possible. For instance, if $U(\tilde{W})$ is quadratic, then $\phi_n = 0$ and $\pi_n \neq 0$ since $\phi = bV$ and $\pi$ is a function of $W$ as well as $V$ (cf. Equations 3.21 and 3.22).

In the example, the relation between return and variance was, of course, the same, independent of whether one used $\phi$ or $\pi$ as the risk measure. The choice of risk measure cannot affect either the optimal solution or the relations between variables. It only influences how one interprets these variables. If, however, one is doing empirical estimation involving behavioral assumptions and approximations to the actual equations, or if one is doing asset selection employing heuristics that involve assumptions about the shape of the efficient locus, then the choice of risk measure could be important.

## 6.3. Homogeneity and Linearity

It is clear from both the analysis of Chapter 5 and the preceding analysis of this chapter that homogeneity of the risk measure is important both for obtaining closed form solutions and for establishing linear risk-return relationships. In the following sections we generalize the idea of homogeneity, relate the homogeneity of the GRM $\phi$ to the homogeneity of the utility function, and determine conditions for the $(W, \pi)$ efficient locus to be linear.

### 6.3.1. Homogeneity and Related Concepts

DEFINITION 6.1. A function $g(x_1, \ldots, x_n)$ will be called *homogeneous to within a constant* if and only if $g(x_1, \ldots, x_n)$ can be written as

$$g(x_1, \ldots, x_n) = \overset{1}{g}(x_1, \ldots, x_n) + c$$

where $\overset{1}{g}(x_1, \ldots, x_n)$ is a homogeneous function and $c$ is a constant.

NOTATION. The symbol $g \in H_c^k$ will be read "$g$ is homogeneous of degree $k$ to within a constant $c$."

DEFINITION 6.2. A function $g(x_1, \ldots, x_n)$ will be called *homogeneous to within a linear transformation* if and only if

$$g(x_1, \ldots, x_n) = \overset{1}{g}(x_1, \ldots, x_n) + \sum_{i=1}^{n} a_i x_i + c$$

where $\overset{1}{g}(x_1, \ldots, x_n) \in H^k$, $\{a_i\}$ and $c$ are constants.

NOTATION. The symbol $g \in H_l^k$ will be read "$g$ is homogeneous of degree $k$ to within a linear transformation."

Clearly, the class of functions homogeneous to within a linear transformation contains the class of functions that are homogeneous to within a constant which in turn contains the class of functions that are homogeneous of degree $k$.

Before proceeding with the analysis, it is necessary to establish an analogue to Euler's theorem for the case of functions homogeneous to within a constant. It is given in the lemma below.

LEMMA 6.1.

$$g(x_1, \ldots, x_n) \in H_c^k \Leftrightarrow \sum_{j=1}^{n} \frac{\partial g}{\partial x_j} x_j = kg - kc.$$

PROOF.

$$g(x_1, \ldots, x_n) \in H_c^k \Leftrightarrow g(x_1, \ldots, x_n) = \overset{1}{g}(x_1, \ldots, x_n) + c$$

$$\Leftrightarrow \frac{\partial g}{\partial x_j} = \frac{\partial \overset{1}{g}}{\partial x_j} \quad \text{for } j = 1, \ldots, n$$

$$\Leftrightarrow \sum_{j=1}^n \frac{\partial g}{\partial x_j} x_j = \sum_{j=1}^n \frac{\partial \overset{1}{g}}{\partial x_j} x_j = k \overset{1}{g}$$

$$\text{since } \overset{1}{g} \in H^k$$

$$\Leftrightarrow \sum_{j=1}^n \frac{\partial g}{\partial x_j} x_j = k(g - c) = kg - kc$$

Q.E.D.

### 6.3.2. The Homogeneity of $\phi$

THEOREM 6.3. If $k \neq 1$ and $U(W) \in H_l^k$, then $\phi \in H^k$.

PROOF. If $U(\tilde{W}) \in H_l^k$, then there are constants $a$ and $b$ such that $U(\tilde{W}) = \overset{1}{U}(\tilde{W}) + a\tilde{W} + b$ where $\overset{1}{U}(\tilde{W}) \in H^k$.

$$\therefore \quad U(\overline{W}) = \overset{1}{U}(\overline{W}) + a\overline{W} + b$$

$$\overline{U} = E[\overset{1}{U}(\tilde{W})] + a\overline{W} + b$$

$$\Rightarrow \phi = U(\overline{W}) - \overline{U} = \overset{1}{U}(\overline{W}) - E[\overset{1}{U}(\tilde{W})]$$

If $k = 1$, $\phi = 0$. If $k \neq 1$, then $\phi \in H^k$ since

$$\phi(kx) = \overset{1}{U}(k\overline{W}) - E[\overset{1}{U}(k\tilde{W})] = k\phi(x).$$

Q.E.D.

This proof has been made easy by the fact that

$$\phi(kx_1, \ldots, kx_2) = U(k\overline{W}) - E[U(k\tilde{W})]. \tag{6.22}$$

Thus, we have been able to study the homogeneity of $\phi$ by studying the homogeneity of a function of a single variable.

The converse of this theorem is not necessarily true. Let $U(W)$ be such that $U(W) = \overset{1}{U}(W) + f(W) + aW + b$ where $\overset{1}{U}(W) \in H^k$ and $f(W) \notin H^k$ for any $k$. If the distribution is such that $E[f(\tilde{W})] = f(\overline{W})$, then $\phi$ will be given by $\phi = U(\overline{W}) - \overline{U} = \overset{1}{U}(\overline{W}) - E[\overset{1}{U}(\tilde{W})]$ and $\phi \in H^k$ even though $U(W) \notin H_l^k$. Of course, this requires a particular distribution with a particular mean $\overline{W}$. If $\phi \in H^k$ for every value of $\overline{W}$, for a fixed class of distributions, then it can be shown that $U(W) \in H_l^k$.

### 6.3.3. Linearity of the $(W, \pi)$ Locus

THEOREM 6.4. If $\pi_n = 0$, then the $(W, \pi)$ locus is linear $\Leftrightarrow \pi \in H_c^k$.

PROOF. If $\pi_n = 0$, then from Equation 6.19, we can derive

$$\sum_{j=1}^{n-1} \pi_j x_j = \overline{W} - (1 + r_n)V_0 \qquad (6.23)$$

1. If the $(W, \pi)$ locus is linear, $k\pi = \overline{W} + \text{const}$ for some $k$

$$\Rightarrow \sum_{j=1}^{n-1} \pi_j x_j = k\pi + \text{const}$$

$\Rightarrow \pi \in H_c^k$ for some $k$.

2. If $\pi \in H_c^k$, then $\displaystyle\sum_{j=1}^{n-1} \pi_j x_j = k(\pi - c)$ by Lemma 6.1

$\Rightarrow k(\pi - c) = \overline{W} - (1 + r_n)V_0$ from Equation 6.23.

Q.E.D.

If the $(W, \pi)$ efficient locus is linear, then so is the $(\rho, \pi/V_0)$ efficient locus. (In general, the $(\rho, \Psi)$ locus is linear $\Leftrightarrow$ the $(W, \psi)$ locus is linear.)

Since $\pi = \overline{W} - U^{-1}(\overline{U})$, where $U^{-1}$ is the inverse of $U$, we see that $\pi \in H_c^k \Leftrightarrow \overline{W} - U^{-1}(\overline{U}) \in H_c^k \Leftrightarrow U^{-1}(\overline{U}) \in H_l^k$. Thus, $\pi$ will be homogeneous to within a constant only if $U^{-1}(\overline{U})$ is homogeneous to within a particular linear transformation. One case in which $\pi$ is homogeneous occurs when $U(W) = -\exp(-cW)$ and the distribution is normal as shown in the previous example.

In general, $\phi \notin H^k$ if $\pi \in H^k$ and conversely. Thus, in general, one cannot have both the $(\overline{W}, \phi)$ and the $(W, \pi)$ efficient loci be linear.

# 7
## Mean-Variance
## Models

The purpose of Chapters 7 and 8 is to investigate existing models of capital-market equilibrium that have been formulated by Sharpe, Lintner, and Mossin. These models are each analyzed from the viewpoint of the general model that has been developed previously. The purpose of this analysis is fourfold: (1) to show that each of these models is a special case of the two-parameter functional representation; (2) to exhibit and analyze particular examples of the general model; (3) to extend, clarify, and interpret the results of the existing models; and (4) to show the relation between each of these three models. The major parts of this chapter correspond to the Sharpe and Lintner models; Chapter 8 treats the Mossin model.

The analysis of the Sharpe model is divided into three main parts. First, the Fama–Sharpe derivation of the relation between risk and return is provided in the framework of the Sharpe model. Then the same result is derived as a special case of the two-parameter functional representation. A general summarizing equation for the Sharpe model is obtained, and from this equation the Fama–Sharpe relation between risk and return is shown to follow. After contrasting the Fama–Sharpe derivation with the general derivation, an explicit solution procedure is developed for the Sharpe model. The formulation of this explicit solution is divided into two parts. First, a solution for the relative investment in risky assets is obtained. Then a procedure for obtaining the explicit optimal solution, including the determination of equilibrium prices, is outlined. Throughout this analysis of the Sharpe model, emphasis is placed on indicating what results depend on the form of the utility function and what results are valid for any utility function.

In the analysis of the Lintner model, a summary equation of personal equilibrium is derived, analyzed, and related to Lintner's work. Price determination in the context of the Lintner treatment is considered. Finally, the relation between the Sharpe and Lintner models is investigated.

### 7.1. Derivation of Relationship between Risk and Return in the Sharpe Model

The following derivations present relationships between risk and return that can be extracted from the Sharpe model. The general structure of these derivations is the same as that presented by Fama [6] in developing the implications of the Sharpe model.

Let the following symbols be used:

$r$ = expected return on the optimal portfolio of risky assets (denoted by $t$ in Figure 7.1).

$w = \sum\limits_{j=1}^{n-1} y_j$ = fraction invested in risky assets.

$\sigma_r$ = the standard deviation of the portfolio of risky assets.

$\sigma_{jk} = \text{cov}(r_j, r_k)$

Then

$$\rho = (1 - w)r_n + wr, \tag{7.1}$$

$$\sigma = w\sigma_r, \quad \text{and} \tag{7.2}$$

$$\frac{d\sigma}{d\rho} = \frac{d\sigma}{dw}\frac{dw}{d\rho} = \frac{\sigma_r}{r - r_n}. \tag{7.3}$$

Let $j$ be any risky asset, and let $t$ be the tangency portfolio. The locus of points $jtj'$ summarizes the $(\rho, \sigma)$ combinations that can be obtained by investing a fraction $v$ in the tangency portfolio $t$ and $1 - v$ in the risky asset $j$. What Sharpe refers to as the "investment opportunity locus" is the efficient frontier of Markowitz if there were no risky asset. It is the set of efficient M-V portfolios. Let $\rho_c$ denote the return expected from a portfolio on $jtj'$. Then

$$\rho_c = (1 - v)r_j + vr. \tag{7.4}$$

When $v = 1$ at equilibrium, the curve $jtj'$ must be tangent to the market line at $t$. This condition is the equilibrium requirement of the Fama–Sharpe model—that every security belong to a portfolio on the market line and be included in such a fashion that marginal rate of exchange $d\sigma_c/d\rho_c$ is equal to the "market rate of exchange" $d\sigma/d\rho$ (cf. Fama [6], pp. 34–35).

Sharpe and Fama used this equilibrium condition

$$\left.\frac{d\sigma_c}{d\rho_c}\right|_{v=1} = \frac{d\sigma}{d\rho} \tag{7.5}$$

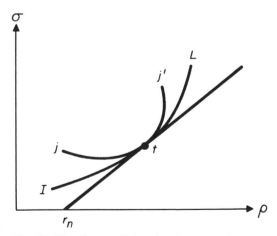

Fig. 7.1. The Sharpe efficient frontier. $IL$ = "investment opportunity locus"; $jj'$ = investment locus corresponding to a linear combination of risky asset $j$ and the tangency portfolio $t$.

to obtain an expression for the expected return in terms of other parameters of the problem. This derivation involves finding an expression for $\sigma_c^2$, the variance of $\rho_c$, evaluating $d\sigma_c/d\rho_c$ at $v = 1$, and substituting this result into the equilibrium condition given by Equation 7.5.

From Equation 7.4, the variance of $\rho_c$ is 44

$$\sigma_c^2 = (1 - v)^2 \sigma_{jj} + 2v(1 - v)\operatorname{cov}(r_j, r) + v^2 \sigma_r^2$$

$$\frac{d\sigma_c^2}{dv} = -2(1 - v)\sigma_{jj} + 2(1 - 2v)\operatorname{cov}(r_j, r) + 2v\sigma_r^2.$$

Using the fact that $d\sigma_c^2/dv = 2\sigma_c(d\sigma_c/dv)$ gives

$$\frac{d\sigma_c}{dv} = \frac{-(1 - v)\sigma_{jj} + (1 - 2v)\operatorname{cov}(r_j, r) + v\sigma_r^2}{\sigma_c}$$

The derivative of $v$ with respect to $\rho_c$ is obtained directly from Equation 7.4. It is $dv/d\rho_c = 1/(r - r_j)$.

Using the chain rule to find $d\sigma_c/d\rho_c$ and evaluating the result at $v = 1$ gives

$$\frac{d\sigma_c}{d\rho_c} = \frac{d\sigma_c}{dv} \cdot \frac{dv}{d\rho_c} = \frac{[-(1 - v)\sigma_{jj} + (1 - 2v)\operatorname{cov}(r_j, r) + v\sigma_r^2]/\sigma_c}{(r - r_j)}$$

$$\Rightarrow \frac{d\sigma_c}{d\rho_c}\bigg|_{v=1} = \frac{-\operatorname{cov}(r_j, r) + \sigma_r^2}{\sigma_r(r - r_j)}$$

where $\sigma_c$ has been replaced by $\sigma_r$ since $\sigma_c|_{v=1} = \sigma_r$. Substituting this result into Equation 7.5 and solving for $r_j$ gives

$$\frac{-\operatorname{cov}(r_j, r) + \sigma_r^2}{\sigma_r(r - r_j)} = \frac{d\sigma}{d\rho} = \frac{\sigma_r}{r - r_n}$$

$$\Rightarrow r_j - r = \frac{r - r_n}{\sigma_r^2}\operatorname{cov}(r_j, r) - (r - r_n)$$

$$\Rightarrow r_j = r_n + \left(\frac{r - r_n}{\sigma_r^2}\right)\operatorname{cov}(r_j, r) \tag{7.6}$$

$$\Rightarrow r_j - r_n = \left(\frac{r - r_n}{\sigma_r^2}\right)\operatorname{cov}(r_j, r) \tag{7.7}$$

Equations 7.6 and 7.7 are Equations 8 and 9, respectively, of Fama [6, p. 35]. Fama shows that Equation 7.7 can be rewritten to obtain Lintner's expression for the risk premium. Writing $r$ in terms of $h_i = y_i/w$, $i = 1, \ldots, n - 1$, where $w = \sum_{i=1}^{n-1} y_i$ is the fraction of wealth invested in risky assets, one has

$$r = \sum_{k=1}^{n-1} r_k h_k$$

$$\text{cov}(r_j, r) = \text{cov}\left(r_j, \sum_{k=1}^{n-1} r_k h_k\right)$$

$$= \sum_{k=1}^{n-1} \text{cov}(r_j, r_k) h_k$$

$$= \sum_{j=1}^{n-1} \sigma_{jk} h_k,$$

and Equation 7.7 becomes

$$r_j - r_n = \frac{r - r_n}{\sigma_r^2} \sum_{k=1}^{n-1} \sigma_{jk} h_k, \tag{7.8}$$

which is the result of Lintner. Equations 7.7 and 7.8 relate the risk premium on an individual security, $r_j - r_n$, to the risk premium on the tangency portfolio $r - r_n$ and the covariances of the risky securities.

Before proceeding with the derivation of the Sharpe model, the structure of the argument involved in the preceding analysis will be summarized and analyzed. The basic steps of the derivation are (1) Sharpe's heuristic argument based on the existence of a riskless asset required that the efficient frontier be linear at equilibrium and, therefore, that the rate of substitution be constant. (2) This constant is the slope of the efficient frontier and is given by $\sigma_r/(r - r_n)$. (3) A tangency condition is established for portfolios consisting of a combination of any risky asset and the "market portfolio." (4) From this tangency requirement, Equations 7.7 and 7.8 were derived.

*Observe that, first, linearity is established, then the slope of efficient frontier is obtained, and only then is an expression for the risk premium derived.* In the following sections, we shall show that both the linearity of the market line and the expression for its slope arise naturally from the expression for the risk premium, which is a direct result of the conditions for *personal equilibrium.*

## 7.2. The Sharpe Model Derived from the Two-Parameter Functional Representation

In the following paragraphs, the two-parameter functional representation will be specialized to obtain the Sharpe model. The results obtained via this specialization of the general model will be contrasted with the results extracted from Sharpe's original heuristic formulation, especially as reformulated by Fama [6] and summarized in the preceding pages.[1]

Sharpe assumed that the utility function for individual $i$ could be represented as[2]

$$U^i = f^i(W^i, S^i) \tag{7.9}$$

where $S^i$ is the standard deviation of future wealth $W^i$.[3] This utility function is a special case of the general two-parameter functional representation with the risk function $\psi^i$ given by

$$\psi^i(x_1^i, \ldots, x_n^i) = S^i(x_1^i, \ldots, x_n^i) = \left( \sum_{j=1}^{n} \sum_{k=1}^{n} S_{jk}^i x_j^i x_k^i \right)^{1/2}, \tag{7.10}$$

where $S_{jk}$ is the covariance of future price of securities $j$ and $k$, i.e.,

$$S_{jk}^i = \text{cov}(\mu_j^i, \mu_k^i).$$

Since the original Sharpe model and all subsequent work relating to it has used return $\rho$ and its standard deviation $\sigma$ as variables, the specialization of the general model will be in terms of return $\rho$ and its standard deviation $\sigma$, where $\sigma$ is the portfolio risk per dollar.

THEOREM 7.1. The major results of the Sharpe model are summarized by the following two equations:

$$\frac{d\sigma^i}{d\rho^i} = \frac{\sigma_j^i}{r_j^i - r_n^i} = \frac{\sum_{j=1}^{n-1} \sigma_j^i y_j^i}{\rho^i - r_n^i} = \frac{\sigma^i}{\rho^i - r_n^i} = \beta^i(\mathbf{p}) \quad j = 1, \ldots, n-1 \tag{7.11}$$

$$\frac{\sigma_j^i}{r_j^i - r_n^i} = \frac{\sigma_k^i}{r_k^i - r_n^i} \quad \text{for every } j, k = 1, \ldots, n-1, \tag{7.12}$$

where $\beta^i(\mathbf{p})$ is a constant for a given set of prices.

Two proofs will be given, the first one based on a specialization of the general results of Chapter 5; the second a direct derivation. The first proof is given to provide an application of the general theory and indicate its power; the second is given to make clear what is involved in the derivation and thereby to facilitate comparison with the results and methods of Sharpe and Fama.

PROOF 1.1. To specialize the general model to the Sharpe model, the risk per dollar $\Psi^i$ must be replaced by $\sigma^i$ and the marginal risk per dollar $\Psi_j^i$ must be

[1] The diagonal model about which Sharpe was particularly concerned will not be considered.
[2] Sharpe [26, p. 428] stated his original utility function in terms of wealth and its standard deviation. However, he changed variables to return and its standard deviation and expressed his utility function in terms of the transformed variables for his analysis. Sharpe justifies the expression of the utility function in terms of return by assuming that the investor's wealth is fixed throughout the analysis.
[3] The notation to be used throughout this chapter is that $S$ will refer to standard deviation of *wealth* and $\sigma$ to the standard deviation of *returns*, i.e., $S^2 = \text{var}(W)$; $\sigma^2 = \text{var}(\rho)$.

replaced by $\sigma_j^i$ in the general equations. $\sigma_j^i$ can be expressed as

$$\sigma_j^i = \frac{d\sigma^i}{dy_j^i} = \frac{\sum_{k=1}^{n-1} \sigma_{jk}^i y_k^i}{\sigma^i}. \tag{7.13}$$

2. From Corollary 5.4.2, Equation 5.33 on the equality of the ratio of marginal risk per dollar to risk premium, we have

$$\frac{\Psi_j^i}{m_j^i} = \frac{\Psi_k^i}{m_k^i} \qquad j, k = 1, \ldots, n-1$$

$$\Rightarrow \frac{\sigma_j^i}{r_j^i - r_n^i} = \frac{\sigma_k^i}{r_k^i - r_n^i} \qquad j, k = 1, \ldots, n-1,$$

which is Equation 7.12.

3. From Equation 5.9 with $\Psi_n^i = 0$ and from Theorem 5.5, Equation 5.34 for the rate of substitution of risk for return we have

$$\frac{d\Psi^i}{d\rho^i} = \frac{\Psi_j^i}{r_j^i - r_n^i} = \frac{\sum_{j=1}^{n-1} \Psi_j^i y_j^i}{\rho^i - r_n^i}$$

$$\Rightarrow \frac{d\sigma^i}{d\rho^i} = \frac{\sigma_j^i}{r_j^i - r_n^i} = \frac{\sum_{j=1}^{n} \sigma_j^i y_j^i}{\rho^i - r_n^i} \tag{A}$$

This last equation is the first part of Equation 7.11.

4. Since $\sigma^i \in H^1$, we have from Theorem 5.6 on homogeneous risk functions that

$$\frac{d\Psi^i}{d\rho^i} = \frac{k\Psi^i}{\rho^i - r_n^i}$$

$$\Rightarrow \frac{d\sigma^i}{d\rho^i} = \frac{\sigma^i}{\rho^i - r_n^i} \quad \text{since } k = 1. \tag{B}$$

From Equation 5.42 of Corollary 5.7.1 for the efficient locus in the $(\rho^i, \Psi^i)$ plane when there is a riskless asset and a homogeneous risk function, we have

$$\Psi^i = \beta^i(\mathbf{p})(\rho - r_n^i)^k \quad \text{when } \Psi^i \in H^k$$

$$\Rightarrow \sigma^i = \beta^i(\mathbf{p})(\rho - r_n^i) \quad \text{since } \sigma^i \in H^1$$

$$\therefore \quad \frac{\sigma^i}{\rho^i - r_n^i} = \beta^i(\mathbf{p}) \tag{C}$$

where $\beta^i(\mathbf{p})$ is a constant for a given set of prices.

6. Combining the specialization of the general results to the Sharpe model that is summarized in Equations (A), (B), and (C), we have

$$\frac{d\sigma^i}{d\rho^i} = \frac{\sigma^i_j}{r^i_j - r^i_n} = \frac{\sum\limits_{j=1}^{n-1} \sigma^i_j y^i_j}{\rho^i - r^i_n} = \frac{\sigma^i}{\rho^i - r^i_n} = \beta^i(\mathbf{p}),$$

which is Equation 7.11.

Q.E.D.

This proof has combined the results of four theorems and their corollaries from the general model to obtain these two summary equations for the Sharpe model. The proof illustrates the ease with which the general model may be used to obtain the properties of a specific model.

The Sharpe model has such a simple structure that the results are also easily obtained from the first-order conditions for maximization of the objective function $f(W, S)$.

PROOF 2. To maximize $f^i(W^i, S^i)$ subject to the constraint

$$\sum_{j=1}^{n} p^i_j x^i_j = \sum_{j=1}^{n} p_j \hat{x}^i_j,$$

form the Lagrangian

$$L^i = f^i(W^i, S^i) - \lambda^i \left[ \sum_{j=1}^{n} p_j(x^i_j - \hat{x}^i_j) \right].$$

The first-order conditions are

$$0 = \frac{\partial L^i}{\partial x^i_j} = f^i_1 \mu^i_j + f^i_2 S^i_j - \lambda^i p_j \quad j = 1, \ldots, n-1$$

$$0 = \frac{\partial L^i}{\partial x^i_n} = f^i_1 \mu^i_n - \lambda^i p_n$$

$$\Rightarrow f^i_1 \left( \frac{\mu^i_j}{p_j} - \frac{\mu^i_n}{p_n} \right) + f^i_2 \frac{S^i_j}{p_j} = 0.$$

(7.14)

$$\therefore \quad f^i_1(r^i_j - r^i_n) + f^i_2 \sigma^i_j = 0$$

(7.15)

since

$$\frac{\mu^i_j}{p_j} - \frac{\mu^i_n}{p_n} = r^i_j - r^i_n \quad \text{and} \quad \frac{S^i_j}{p_j} = \sigma^i_j.$$

Solving Equation 7.15 for $-(f_1^i/f_2^i)$ gives

$$\frac{d\sigma^i}{d\rho^i} = -\frac{f_1^i}{f_2^i} = \frac{\sigma_j^i}{r_j^i - r_n^i} \qquad j = 1, \ldots, n-1 \tag{D}$$

$$\therefore \quad \frac{d\sigma^i}{d\rho^i} = \frac{\sigma_j^i y_j^i}{r_j^i y_j^i - r_n^i y_n^i} = \frac{\sum\limits_{j=1}^{n} \sigma_j^i y_j^i}{\rho - r_n^i} \qquad \text{since } \sum\limits_{j=1}^{n} y_j^i = 1, \tag{E}$$

where the method of ratio addition has been used. Using the fact that $\sigma^i \in H^1$ and applying Euler's theorem gives

$$\frac{d\sigma^i}{d\rho^i} = \frac{\sigma^i}{\rho^i - r_n^i}. \tag{F}$$

Combining Equations (D), (E), and (F), gives Equation 7.11:

$$\frac{d\sigma^i}{d\rho^i} = \frac{\sigma_j^i}{r_j^i - r_n^i} = \frac{\sum\limits_{j=1}^{n} \sigma_j^i y_j^i}{\rho^i - r_n^i} = \frac{\sigma^i}{\rho^i - r_n^i}.$$

Since the left-hand side of Equation (D) is independent of the subscript $j$, it follows that

$$\frac{\sigma_j^i}{r_j^i - r_n^i} = \frac{\sigma_k^i}{r_k^i - r_n^i},$$

which is Equation 7.12. Solution of the differential equation given by Equation (F) establishes that $d\sigma^i/d\rho^i$ is a constant.

Q.E.D.

Observe that in the proof, the order in which the results of Equation 7.11 were established is the order in which they are written. Only the existence of a riskless asset was required to establish the first two parts (Equations D and E), but homogeneity of the risk function was also required to establish Equation F.

Equation 7.12 requires only the existence of a riskless asset and does not require homogeneity. That an individual expects the ratio of the marginal risk to risk premium to be the same for each security is a general property of personal equilibrium requiring only the existence of a riskless asset.

Equations 7.7 and 7.8, the Sharpe–Lintner–Fama equation relating risk premium to risk in equilibrium, follows directly from Equation 7.11. This fact is proved in the following corollary.

Let the superscripts denoting individual $i$'s expectations be dropped for the moment, but keep in mind that such an equation can be developed for *each* individual.

COROLLARY 7.1.1. Equation 7.11 implies the Fama–Lintner–Sharpe expression for the risk premium, i.e.,

$$\frac{\sigma_j}{r_j - r_n} = \frac{\sigma}{\rho - r_n} \text{ (Equation 7.11)}$$

$$\Rightarrow r_j - r_n = \frac{r - r_n}{\sigma_r^2} \sum_{k=1}^{n-1} \sigma_{jk} h_k = \frac{r - r_n}{\sigma_r^2} \text{cov}(r_j, r).$$

This expression is the Fama–Sharpe equation for the risk premium (see Equations 7.7 and 7.8). It follows directly from the summary equation of the Sharpe model given in Theorem 7.1.

PROOF.

$$\frac{\sigma_j}{r_j - r_n} = \frac{\sigma}{\rho - r_n}$$

$$\Rightarrow r_j - r_n = \frac{\rho - r_n}{\sigma} \sigma_j = \frac{\rho - r_n}{\sigma^2} \sum_{k=1}^{n-1} \sigma_{jk} y_k, \tag{7.16}$$

since $\sigma_j = \dfrac{\displaystyle\sum_{k=1}^{n-1} \sigma_{jk} y_k}{\sigma}$.

Changing variables from $y_j$ to $h_j = y_j/w$ leads to

$$\frac{\rho - r_n}{\sigma^2} \sum_{j=1}^{n-1} \sigma_{jk} y_k = \frac{w(r - r_n)}{w^2 \sigma_r^2} \sum_{k=1}^{n-1} \sigma_{jk}(w h_k) = \frac{r - r_n}{\sigma_r^2} \sum_{k=1}^{n-1} \sigma_{jk} h_k, \tag{7.17}$$

since $\rho - r_n = w(r - r_n)$ and $\sigma^2 = w^2 \sigma_r^2$.

Thus, substituting Equation 7.17 into Equation 7.16 gives Equation 7.8, i.e.,

$$r_j - r_n = \frac{r - r_n}{\sigma_r^2} \sum_{k=1}^{n-1} \sigma_{jk} h_k.$$

Substituting $\text{cov}(r_j, r)$ for $\displaystyle\sum_{k=1}^{n-1} \sigma_{jk} h_k$ gives Equation 7.7, i.e.,

$$r_j - r_n = \frac{r - r_n}{\sigma_r^2} \text{cov}(r_j, r).$$

Q.E.D.

Thus, it has been established that the Fama–Sharpe result can be obtained directly from Equation 7.11, the summary equation for the Sharpe model as a special case of the two-parameter functional representation.[4]

Now that it has been established that the Fama–Sharpe result can be extracted from Equation 7.11, we consider the converse question: Can the new results of the Sharpe model summarized in Equations 7.11 and 7.12 be extracted from Equation 7.7? The answer is yes, but only *if* one makes the additional assumption that the efficient frontier is linear.

COROLLARY 7.1.2. If it is assumed that the efficient frontier is linear, then the Fama–Sharpe equation implies Theorem 7.1, i.e.,

$$
\left.
\begin{array}{l}
1. \ r_j - r_n = \dfrac{r - r_n}{\sigma_r^2} \displaystyle\sum_{k=1}^{n-1} \sigma_{jk} h_k \\[2em]
\text{and} \\[1em]
2. \ \text{A linear efficient frontier}
\end{array}
\right\}
\Rightarrow
\left\{
\begin{array}{l}
\dfrac{d\sigma}{d\rho} = \dfrac{\sigma_j}{r_j - r_n} = \dfrac{\sigma}{\rho - r_n} = \beta \\[2em]
\dfrac{\sigma_j}{r_j - r_n} = \dfrac{\sigma_k}{r_k - r_n} \ \text{for every } j, k
\end{array}
\right.
$$

PROOF. From Equation 7.17,

$$
\frac{r - r_n}{\sigma_r^2} \sum_{k=1}^{n-1} \sigma_{jk} h_k = \frac{\rho - r_n}{\sigma^2} \sum_{j=1}^{n-1} \sigma_{jk} y_k = \frac{\rho - r_n}{\sigma} \sigma_j
$$

since $\sigma_j = \dfrac{\displaystyle\sum_{k=1}^{n-1} \sigma_{jk} y_k}{\sigma}$.

Therefore,

$$
r_j - r_n = \frac{r - r_n}{\sigma_r^2} \sum_{j=1}^{n-1} \sigma_{jk} = \frac{\rho - r_n}{\sigma} \sigma_j
$$

$$
\Rightarrow \frac{r_j - r_n}{\sigma_j} = \frac{\rho - r_n}{\sigma}.
$$

Since $(r - r_n)/\sigma_r = (\rho - r_n)/\sigma$ and since the Fama–Sharpe model obtains $d\sigma/d\rho = \sigma_r/(r - r_n)$ as part of the argument that the efficient frontier must be linear, it follows that Equation 7.11 holds, i.e.,

$$
\frac{d\sigma}{d\rho} = \frac{\sigma_r}{r - r_n} = \frac{\sigma}{\rho - r_n} = \frac{\sigma_j}{r_j - r_n}.
$$

---

[4] Corollary 7.1.1 may also be regarded as a special case of Corollary 5.1.4 for the TPFR; the proof may be based on a direct specialization of the general results of this corollary to the Sharpe model. See Section 7.2.1 for a more thorough treatment of this idea.

Again the fact that the left-hand side is independent of the subscript $j$ implies that

$$\frac{\sigma_j}{r_j - r_n} = \frac{\sigma_k}{r_k - r_n} \quad \text{for } j, k = 1, \ldots, n - 1$$

Q.E.D.

Thus, it has been established that both versions of the Sharpe model give the same results although many of the implications of the model had not been extracted from the Fama–Sharpe version of the model. The major differences in the models lies in the logical structure of the derivations and their natural interpretation.

In the Fama–Sharpe derivation, it is first argued that at equilibrium, the efficient frontier must be linear and that the rate of substitution of risk for return must, therefore, be constant. Crucial to this argument is the idea of the market portfolio or tangency portfolio, the existence of a riskless asset, and the fact that wealth invested is independent of both the available opportunities and any adjustment in these opportunities that occurs when the market is out of equilibrium.[5] From the argument of a linear efficient frontier, the tangency criterion for a portfolio consisting of a combination of any risky asset and the market portfolio is introduced and, from this tangency criterion, the Fama–Sharpe expression for the risk premium is derived. Only after this equation has been obtained can the summary equations given in Theorem 7.1 be derived; moreover, their derivation requires that the linearity of the efficient frontier be assumed.

When the implications of the Sharpe model are derived in the context of the general model, one immediately establishes the fundamental result that the rate of substitution of risk for return is equal to the ratio of marginal risk, $\sigma_j$, to risk premium, $r_j - r_n$, for each security. Then from this relationship and the homogeneity of standard deviation, one establishes that $d\sigma/d\rho = \sigma/(\rho - r_n)$ and that the solution set is in fact a line with an intercept on the $\rho$-axis of $r_n$. *In this derivation, the linearity of the solution set arises naturally from the mathematics; it is not the starting point from which other (more basic) results are derived.*

In addition to presenting the implications of the model in logically more direct and mathematically compact form, this model facilitates interpretation. To illustrate the interpretative power, we will compare the interpretations of the model given by Fama with the interpretations implied by the development presented here.

---

[5] Note that no use is made of the fact that standard deviation is homogeneous of degree although this is the crucial fact necessary to establish the linearity of the market curve as shown in Chapter 5.

### 7.2.1. The Measure of Security Risk. Fama interpreted Equations 7.7 and 7.8 by writing them as

$$r_j - r_n = \lambda \sum_{j=1}^{n-1} \sigma_{jk} h_k = \lambda \operatorname{cov}(r_j, r),$$

where

$$\lambda \equiv \frac{r - r_n}{\sigma_r^2} = \frac{1}{\sigma_r} \left( \frac{d\rho}{d\sigma} \right)_p.$$

From this Fama asserted that the risk premium was proportional to the weighted average of the covariance of security $j$ with each other security at equilibrium.[6] The result can be reinterpreted as follows:

$$r_j - r_n = \lambda \sum_{j=1}^{n-1} \sigma_{jk} h_k = \frac{r - r_n}{\sigma_r} \frac{\sum_{k=1}^{n-1} \sigma_{jk} h_k}{\sigma} = \frac{dr}{d\sigma_r} \sigma_j;$$

recognizing that $(\Sigma_k \sigma_{jk} h_k)/\sigma_r = \sigma_j$ is the marginal risk of the portfolio of risky assets[7] and identifying marginal portfolio risk with security risk, we have for the Sharpe model

$$\text{risk premium} = \frac{d \text{ (return)}}{d \text{ (risk)}} \cdot (\text{security risk})$$

This expression is a special case of the general result given by Equation 5.20 for the TPFR in which we have

$$\Delta \text{ (return)} = \frac{d \text{ (return)}}{d \text{ (risk)}} \cdot \Delta \text{ (security risk)},$$

where the security risk of asset $n$ is zero.

Writing the risk premium as $\lambda \sum_{k=1}^{n} \sigma_{jk} h_k$ has resulted in a failure to recognize the basic structure of the expression for the risk premium. The measure of security risk has been regarded as a weighted sum of covariances and not marginal risk *per se*. The fact that standard deviation is the measure of risk in the models of Lintner, Sharpe, and Fama means that marginal risk will be related to (but not equal to!) this weighted sum of covariances. Moreover,

---

[6] See Fama [6], pp. 35–36.
[7] This expression is the marginal portfolio risk since

$$\frac{\sum_{k=1}^{n-1} \sigma_{jk} h_k}{\sigma_r} = \frac{\sum_{k=1}^{n-1} \sigma_{jk} y_k}{\sigma} = \frac{d\sigma}{dy_j} = \frac{dS}{dx_j}.$$

regarding $(1/\sigma_r)/(dr/d\sigma)$ as the proportionality constant obscures the role of $d\sigma/d\rho$ as the rate of exchange between risk and return.

**7.2.2. Weighted Sums.** Fama [6, p. 36] correctly observed that the *variance* of the risky portfolio was the weighted average of *his* measure of risk, $\text{cov}(r_j, r)$, the weights being the relative position in the risk portfolio, i.e.,

$$\sigma_r^2 = \sum_{j=1}^{n-1} h_j \, \text{cov}(r_j, r).$$

If, however, the marginal risk, $\sigma_j = \text{cov}(r_j, r)/\sigma_r$, replaces $\text{cov}(r_j, r)$ in the weighted sum, the result becomes standard deviation of the risky portfolio, i.e.,

$$\sum_{j=1}^{n-1} h_j \frac{\text{cov}(r_j, r)}{\sigma_r} = \frac{\sigma_r^2}{\sigma_r} = \sigma_r.$$

Hence, in the Sharpe model the weighted sum of the measure of risk of an individual asset is the measure of risk for the entire risky portfolio (and not the square of the risk as the Fama interpretation would indicate). Moreover, the reason that the measure of the risk of the portfolio of risky assets is the weighted sum of the risk of the individual assets is that the risk measure is homogeneous.[8]

Thus, from the viewpoint of the general model, we are able not only to reformulate meaningfully the Fama observation, but we are able to explain the result as a basic property of a homogeneous measure of risk.

**7.2.3. The Tangency Criterion and Equilibrium.** So far the analysis of the Sharpe model has been restricted to a consideration of personal equilibrium. No market-clearing requirement has been invoked. Theorem 7.1 and its corollaries are descriptions of personal equilibrium.

It has been established that Theorem 7.1 implies the basic Fama–Sharpe equation (see Equations 7.7 and 7.8) and that *if* one also assumes the efficient frontier is linear, the Fama–Sharpe equation implies Theorem 7.1. Thus, the

---

[8] The equivalence of this result to the homogeneity of $\sigma$ is here proved.

CLAIM. $\displaystyle\sum_{j=1}^{n-1} h_j\sigma_j = \sigma_r \Leftrightarrow \sum_{j=1}^{n-1} y_j\sigma_j = \sigma.$

PROOF. $\displaystyle\sum_{j=1}^{n-1} h_j\sigma_j = \sigma_r \Leftrightarrow \sum_{j=1}^{n-1} (wh_j)\sigma_j = w\sigma_r \Leftrightarrow \sum_{j=1}^{n-1} y_j\sigma_j = \sigma$

since $y_j = wh_j$ and $\sigma = w\sigma_r$.

Q.E.D.

*Fama–Sharpe equation is a description of personal equilibrium for an individual investor valid for any set of prices facing the investors.* This means that the tangency criterion upon which the derivation is based is actually a condition for personal equilibrium.

Once it is recognized that the tangency requirement is only a condition of personal equilibrium, it is easy to relate it to the first-order conditions of a utility maximizer. The tangency conditions require that all securities have the same rate of exchange, and from the reformulation of the Sharpe model that is summarized in Theorem 7.1 we know that this requires that all securities have the same ratio of marginal risk to risk compensation, i.e.,

$$\frac{\sigma_j}{r_j - r_n} = \text{const} = \frac{\sigma_k}{r_k - r_n},$$

where the constant is the rate of exchange.

The fact that the tangency criterion is a condition of personal equilibrium and not by itself a condition of market equilibrium is significant. It means that the linearity of the efficient frontier (or, more precisely, the efficient locus) is a property of personal equilibrium. Moreover, a market equilibrium model based on the tangency criterion must, to be complete, also include a market-clearing requirement.[9]

To summarize this discussion of measures of risk, we prove the following corollaries of Theorem 7.1.

COROLLARY 7.1.3. In the Sharpe model, two risky securities will have the same return if and only if they have the same marginal risk, i.e., $r_i = r_k \Leftrightarrow \sigma_j = \sigma_k$ where $\sigma_j = d\sigma/dy_j$.

PROOF. $r_j - r_n = \left(\dfrac{d\rho}{d\sigma}\right)_{\text{P}} \sigma_j$ from Equation 7.11;

$\therefore \quad r_j = r_k \Leftrightarrow \sigma_j = \sigma_k.$

Q.E.D.

COROLLARY 7.1.4. In the Sharpe model, security $j$ will have a greater return than security $k$ if and only if the marginal risk of security $j$ is greater than the marginal risk of security $k$, i.e.,

$r_j > r_k \Leftrightarrow \sigma_j > \sigma_k.$

[9] Additional aspects of the distinction between personal and market equilibrium are contained in Section 7.3, "The Market Equilibrium Solution of the Sharpe Model."

PROOF. From Equation 7.11 we have

$$\begin{cases} r_j - r_n = \dfrac{\sigma_j}{\beta} \\[2mm] r_k - r_n = \dfrac{\sigma_k}{\beta} \end{cases}$$

$$\therefore \quad r_j > r_k \Leftrightarrow \sigma_j > \sigma_k.$$

Q.E.D.

The implication of this result is that all securities may be ranked according to their riskiness by ranking them according to their return.[10]

COROLLARY 7.1.5. The return on a risky asset will be less than the return on the riskless asset if and only if the risky asset has a negative marginal risk.

PROOF. $r_j - r_n = \sigma_j/\beta$ from Equation 7.11.

$$\frac{1}{\beta} = \frac{\rho - r_n}{\sigma} > 0 \quad \text{since } \sigma > 0 \text{ and } \rho > r_n;$$

$$\therefore \quad r_j - r_n < 0 \Leftrightarrow \sigma_j < 0$$

$$\therefore \quad r_j < r_n \Leftrightarrow \sigma_j < 0.$$

Q.E.D.

### 7.3. The Market-Equilibrium Solution of the Sharpe Model
Recall that the market-equilibrium solution to the asset-selection problem involves specification of each individual's holdings of each security and the price of each security that produces market clearing.

In this section we shall first solve for the relative investment in risky assets as a function of prices, and we shall investigate the properties of this solution. We express the slope of the efficient frontier as a function of prices and given parameters. Then we show how the scale of investment is determined once the form of the utility function is specified and indicate how the prices that produce market clearing and the complete market-equilibrium solution are obtained.

**7.3.1. The Portfolio of Risky Assets.** THEOREM 7.2. If the covariance matrix $\Sigma$ of risky assets is nonsingular, then the relative investment in risky assets is given by

$$\mathbf{h} = \frac{\Sigma^{-1} \cdot \mathbf{m}}{\mathbf{1}' \cdot \Sigma^{-1} \cdot \mathbf{m}} \tag{7.18}$$

[10] Note, however, that this ranking is based on *expected* return (and is not necessarily related to *realized* return) and is primarily a property of personal equilibrium.

where

$\mathbf{h} = [h_1, \ldots, h_{n-1}]$ is the vector describing the relative investment in risky assets

$\mathbf{m} = [m_1, \ldots, m_{n-1}]$ is the vector of risk premiums

$\mathbf{1} = [1, \ldots, 1]$ is a constant $(n - 1) \times 1$ vector consisting entirely of 1's

$\Sigma^{-1}$ = inverse of the covariance matrix.

To prove this theorem we shall first make a (nonlinear) change of variables to linearize Equation 7.8.[11] Then we will solve the linear equation and transform back to the original variables. Vector notation will be used to provide compactness.

PROOF. Introduce a variable transformation by defining a new variable $u_k$ as

$$u_k = \left( \frac{r - r_n}{\sigma_r^2} \right) h_k$$

Then Equation 7.8 can be rewritten as

$$m_j = r_j - r_n = \frac{r - r_n}{\sigma_r^2} \sum_{k=1}^{n-1} \sigma_{jk} h_k = \sum_{k=1}^{n-1} \sigma_{jk} u_k.$$

In vector notation, this can be rewritten as

$$\mathbf{m} = \Sigma \cdot \mathbf{u}$$

$$\Rightarrow \mathbf{u} = \Sigma^{-1} \cdot \mathbf{m} \tag{7.19}$$

Since $\sum_{k=1}^{n-1} h_k = 1$, $h_k$ can be written as

$$h_k = \frac{u_k}{\sum\limits_{k=1}^{n-1} u_k}. \tag{7.20}$$

In vector notation this becomes

$$\mathbf{h} = \frac{\mathbf{u}}{\mathbf{1}' \cdot \mathbf{u}}$$

Substituting from Equation 7.18, the solution for $\mathbf{h}$ is given by

$$\mathbf{h} = \frac{\mathbf{u}}{\mathbf{1}' \cdot \mathbf{u}} = \frac{\Sigma^{-1} \cdot \mathbf{m}}{\mathbf{1}' \cdot \Sigma^{-1} \cdot \mathbf{m}}$$

Q.E.D.

[11] The use of this transformation as a means of solving for $\mathbf{h}$ is due to Lintner [15].

Observe that **h** is expressed in terms of the covariance matrix and the vector of risk premiums, both of which depend on prices and known parameters. The dependence of $\Sigma$ on prices is indicated in Lemma 7.1. Allowing for differences in expectations, Equation 7.18 becomes

$$\mathbf{h}^i = \frac{(\Sigma^i)^{-1} \cdot \mathbf{m}^i}{\mathbf{1}' \cdot (\Sigma^i)^{-1} \cdot \mathbf{m}^i} \tag{7.21}$$

LEMMA 7.1. The covariance of future prices and the covariance of future returns are related by

$$\sigma_{jk} = \frac{S_{jk}}{p_j p_k}$$

PROOF.

$$\sigma_{jk} \equiv \mathrm{cov}(r_j, r_k) = \mathrm{cov}\left(\frac{\mu_j}{p_j} - 1, \frac{\mu_k}{p_k} - 1\right)$$

$$= \frac{\mathrm{cov}(\mu_j, \mu_k)}{p_j p_k} = \frac{S_{jk}}{p_j p_k}$$

Q.E.D.

Note that the derivation of Equation 7.18 depends only on properties of personal equilibrium and is independent of the form of an investor's utility function. Thus, Equation 7.18 is valid for any given set of prices as long as $\Sigma$ is nonsingular;[12] however, it is an equilibrium solution only when prices are such that the market is cleared.

We shall now investigate attributes of an individual's holdings of risky assets.

COROLLARY 7.2.1. When there is complete agreement among investors about security parameters, **h** is the same for all investors and thus all investors will hold the same portfolio of risky assets. Individuals will differ only in the fraction of their wealth $w$ that they invest in risky assets.

The proof of this corollary follows directly from the theorem, since $\mathbf{h}^i$ depends only on $\Sigma$ and **m** and not on individual $i$'s utility function. Thus all individuals will seek to hold the same securities in the same relative amounts. This interpretation of **h** is similar to that provided by Sharpe in his geometrical derivation of the tangency portfolio.

---

[12] When $\Sigma$ is singular, then there are not enough independent equations to uniquely specify **h**. In this case there is not a unique relative investment in risky assets. Note that it is possible, although not likely, for $\Sigma$ to be made singular by price adjustment even when S is nonsingular.

The fact that all investors hold the same portfolio of risky assets suggests that all securities must belong to the market portfolio in order to achieve market clearing. The following two corollaries examine other properties of security holdings in the so-called market portfolio.

COROLLARY 7.2.2. The ratio of each individual's holdings of two risky securities is equal to the ratio of the current market value of the two securities at market equilibrium, i.e.,

$$\frac{h_j}{h_k} = \frac{p_j X_j}{p_k X_k},$$ (7.22)

where

$$X_j = \sum_{i=1}^{m} x_j^i = \text{the total outstanding stock of company } j$$

$p_j X_j = $ the current market value of company $j$.

PROOF. By definition of $h_j$ and $h_k$, we have

$$\frac{h_j}{h_k} = \frac{y_j^i}{y_k^i} = \frac{p_j x_j^i}{p_k x_k^i},$$ (7.23)

where superscripts have been placed on $y$ and $x$ to denote that different individuals will in general have different holdings of the riskless asset and, therefore, of $y$ and $x$; superscripts have been omitted from $h$ since all $h$ are the same for all individuals when there is complete agreement. Using the method of ratio addition, Equation 7.23 becomes

$$\frac{h_j}{h_k} = \frac{p_j \sum_{i=1}^{m} x_j^i}{p_k \sum_{i=1}^{m} x_k^i} = \frac{p_j X_j}{p_k X_k}.$$

Q.E.D.

Note that the market-clearing equations were invoked in the last step of this proof. Therefore, this corollary is valid only at market equilibrium. It is not just a property of personal equilibrium.

COROLLARY 7.2.3. In the Sharpe model, each individual holds the *same* fraction of the outstanding shares of each security, i.e.,

$$\frac{x_j^i}{X_j} = \frac{x_k^i}{X_k} \quad \text{for} \quad \begin{matrix} i = 1, \ldots, m \\ j, k = 1, \ldots, n-1 \end{matrix}$$ (7.24)

PROOF. Equations 7.22 and 7.23 are

$$\frac{h_j}{h_k} = \frac{p_j X_j}{p_k X_k}$$

$$\frac{h_j}{h_k} = \frac{p_j x_j^i}{p_k x_k^i}$$

$$\Rightarrow \frac{x_j^i}{X_j} = \frac{x_k^i}{X_k}$$

Q.E.D.

Both Corollary 7.2.2 and Corollary 7.2.3 require complete agreement for their proof. When the assumption of complete agreement is dropped, the expression for $\mathbf{h}^i$ implied by the conditions of personal equilibrium for individual $i$ is no longer the same for each individual. Then, Equation 7.21 must be used, and it is no longer true that $h_k^i = h_k^j$. The expression for the ratio of an individual's investment in risky assets becomes

$$\frac{h_j^i}{h_k^i} = \frac{y_j^i}{y_k^i} = \frac{p_j x_j^i}{p_k x_k^i}.$$

Now it is no longer possible to use the method of ratio addition to sum the numerator and denominator over $i$, since the left-hand side of this equation is different for different $i$. Equations 7.22 and 7.24 are no longer valid.

To summarize the properties of the risky portfolio, it has been established that complete agreement model implies (1) All individuals hold the same portfolio of risky assets. (2) The ratio of each individual's holdings of two risky assets is equal to their market value. (3) Each individual holds the same proportion of the outstanding stock of each risky security. Additional facts about the portfolio of risky assets under complete agreement at market equilibrium are (4) Each individual holds some of each security. (5) No individual is short in any security. (6) Each risky security belongs to the market portfolio. The last three facts follow directly from the market-clearing requirements and will not be proved.

The first property is a personal-equilibrium relationship; the remaining properties all require market clearing and are thus valid only at market equilibrium. The solution for $\mathbf{h}$ (and consequently, properties 1 to 6 of the portfolio of risky assets) do not depend on the particular form of the utility function.[13] However, as will be proved in the next section, specification of both

[13] That is, the particular form of an admissible utility function; it must possess a constrained maximum and satisfy the continuity properties stated in Chapter 4.

the scale of investment and the equilibrium prices does depend on the form of each individual's utility function.

**7.3.2. The Complete Solution of the Sharpe Model.**[14] Equation 7.18 is a solution for **h**, the relative investment in risky assets. This solution expressed **h** in terms of the covariance matrix $\Sigma$ and the vector of risk premiums **m** which are both functions of prices; symbolically, we have $\mathbf{h} = \mathbf{h(p)}$.

Before proceeding, let us define the notation that will be used in this section. To represent the fact that "The variable $y$ is a function of $x$," we shall write

$$y = y(x). \tag{7.25}$$

If $x$ is a function of two other variables, say, $u$ and $v$, then $y$ is also a function of $u$ and $v$ through its dependence on $x$. To represent this fact that "$y$ is a function of $u$ and $v$," we shall write

$$y = y(u, v), \tag{7.26}$$

where the form of the functional dependence in Equations 7.25 and 7.26 is different. No notational distinction is made to reflect this difference in the form of the function; this notation merely reflects functional dependence and not functional form.[15] This notation for expressing functional dependence is adopted to simplify notation. It avoids the need for creating new functions to represent functional dependence.

The notation $\mathbf{h(p)}$ then should be read, "The vector **h** is a function of the vector **p**."

Now that the notation for functional dependence has been developed, we return to the development of the complete solution of the Sharpe model. The general outline of this development is to show how, once $\mathbf{h(p)}$ is known, the equilibrium equations lead to a determination of the scale of investment in risky assets as a function of prices, and then to an expression for $x_j^i(\mathbf{p})$. Once $x_j^i(\mathbf{p})$ is known, the market-clearing equations lead to a solution for the (relative) prices which produce market clearing. We now proceed with a detailed development of this solution procedure.[16]

Although the solution for **h** is independent of the form of the utility function, the scale of investment in risky assets depends on the form of $f$. The solution for the $n - 1$ components of **h** was obtained from $n - 1$ equations that were obtained from the first-order conditions for personal equilibrium by using the

[14] The material in this section is a specialization to the Sharpe model of the discussion presented in Section 5.5, "The Market Equilibrium Solution."

[15] The conventional notation for the above would be, if $y = f(x)$ and $x = g(u, v)$, then $y = f(x) = f(g(u, v)) = F(u, v)$, where $f$ and $F$ are different functional forms.

[16] We shall express variables as functions of prices; the fact that the system is homogeneous of degree zero in prices means that relative prices could be used as well.

$n$th equation (corresponding to the riskless asset) to eliminate the marginal utility of wealth (the Lagrange multiplier) from the first $n - 1$ equations. To get $w^i(\mathbf{p})$, the fraction of wealth invested in risky assets as a function of prices, one must return to the original system of equations.

By definition of $x_j^i$ and use of the wealth constraint, we have for $j = 1, \ldots, n - 1$ that

$$x_j^i = \frac{y_j^i V_0^i}{p_j} = \frac{h_j^i(w^i V_0^i)}{p_j} \quad \text{since } y_j^i = w^i h_j^i. \tag{7.27}$$

Since $\mathbf{h} = \mathbf{h}(\mathbf{p})$, we have from Equation 7.27 that

$$x_j^i = x_j^i(w^i, \mathbf{p}) \quad j = 1, \ldots, n - 1. \tag{7.28}$$

Thus, once $h_j(\mathbf{p})$ is known, $x_j^i$ is known as a function of $w^i$ and $p_j$ for $j = 1, \ldots, n - 1$.[17] The wealth constraint can be used to express $x_n^i$ as a function of prices and known parameters. This gives

$$x_n^i = \frac{\sum\limits_{k=1}^{n} p_k \hat{x}_k^i - \sum\limits_{k=1}^{n-1} p_k x_k^i}{p_n} = x_n^i(w^i, \mathbf{p}), \tag{7.29}$$

where it will be recalled $\hat{x}_k^i$ is a given parameter and $x_k^i$ for $k \neq n$ is known as a function of $w^i$ and prices.

Using the equation for $x_j^i$ given by Equations 7.28 and 7.29, expected future wealth $W^i$ and its standard deviation $S^i$ can be expressed as functions of only

---

[17] Equation 7.27 can be rewritten as

$$x_j^i = \frac{\left( \sum\limits_{k=1}^{n-1} q_k x_k^i \right) h_j^i}{q_j} \quad j = 1, \ldots, n - 1, \tag{7.27'}$$

since $w^i V_0^i = \sum\limits_{k=1}^{n-1} p_k x_k^i$. This is a set of $n - 1$ equations in the relative prices $\mathbf{q} = (q_1, \ldots, q_{n-1})$; however, it cannot be used to specify $x_j^i = x_j^i(\mathbf{q})$ because the equations are not independent. To prove that these equations are not independent, rewrite Equation 7.27' as

$$h_j^i = \frac{q_j x_j^i}{\sum\limits_{j=1}^{n-1} q_j x_j^i} = \frac{p_j x_j^i}{\sum\limits_{j=1}^{n-1} p_j x_j^i}. \tag{7.27''}$$

Summing Equation 7.27'' from $j = 1$ to $j = n - 1$ gives

$$\sum\limits_{j=1}^{n-1} h_j^i = 1,$$

which is identically true.

$w^i$ and $\mathbf{p}$, since

$$W^i = \sum_{j=1}^{n} \mu_j^i x_j^i(w^i, \mathbf{p}) = W^i(w^i, \mathbf{p})$$

$$S^i = \left[ \sum_{j=1}^{n-1} \sum_{k=1}^{n-1} S_{jk}^i x_j^i(w^i, \mathbf{p}) x_k^i(w^i, \mathbf{p}) \right]^{1/2} = S^i(w^i, \mathbf{p}).$$

This means that $f^i(W^i, S^i)$ and its derivatives $f_1^i$ and $f_2^i$ can be expressed as functions of $w^i$ and $\mathbf{p}$. Thus the first-order condition that corresponds to the riskless asset can be written as

$$f_1^i(w^i, \mathbf{p})\mu_n^i = \lambda^i p_n.$$

Since this equation involves only $w^i$ and $\lambda^i$, it can (in theory at least) be solved to give $\lambda^i$ as a function of $w^i$ and prices, which can be denoted symbolically as

$$\lambda^i = \lambda^i(w^i, \mathbf{p}).$$

This expression can in turn be substituted into any of the other first-order conditions, say the $j$th, to give

$$f_1^i(w^i, \mathbf{p})\mu_j^i + f_2^i(w^i, \mathbf{p})S_j^i(w^i, \mathbf{p}) = \lambda^i(w^i, \mathbf{p})p_j.$$

And this expression can be solved to give $w^i$ as a function of prices alone, i.e., $w^i = w^i(\mathbf{p})$. Once $w^i(\mathbf{p})$ is known, this expression can be substituted into Equations 7.28 and 7.29 to express $x_j^i$ as a function of prices alone, i.e.,

$$x_j^i = x_j^i(w^i, \mathbf{p}) \rightarrow x_j^i(\mathbf{p}). \tag{7.30}$$

Once $x_j^i$ is expressed as a function of only prices and given parameters, the market-clearing conditions can be invoked to provide a set of $n - 1$ equations in the $n - 1$ relative prices,[18] i.e.,

$$\sum_{i=1}^{m} x_j^i(\mathbf{p}) = X_j \quad j = 1, \dots, n - 1,$$

where

$$X_j \equiv \sum_{i=1}^{m} \hat{x}_j^i \quad \text{is known.}$$

The $n - 1$ equations may be solved to provide the $n - 1$ prices of the risky assets relative to the $n$th asset.

[18] The $n$th market-clearing equation has been omitted to account for redundancy.

To summarize, using the symbolic notation employed throughout this section, the complete solution of the Sharpe model involves the following steps:

1. Solve for $\mathbf{h} = \mathbf{h}(\mathbf{p})$.
2. Use this expression to obtain

$$x_j^i = x_j^i(w^i, \mathbf{p}) \qquad j = 1, \ldots, n - 1.$$

3. Use the wealth constraint to obtain

$$x_n^i = x_n^i(w^i, \mathbf{p}).$$

4. Use these expressions for $x_j^i(w^i, \mathbf{p})$ to obtain $f_1^i$ and $f_2^i$ as functions of $w^i$ and $\mathbf{p}$, i.e.,

$$f_1^i(x_1^i, \ldots, x_n^i) \to f_1^i(w^i, \mathbf{p})$$

$$f_2^i(x_1^i, \ldots, x_n^i) \to f_2^i(w^i, \mathbf{p}).$$

5. Use the first-order condition corresponding to the riskless asset, $f_1^i(w^i, \mathbf{p})\mu_n^i = \lambda^i p_n$, to obtain $\lambda^i = \lambda^i(w^i, \mathbf{p})$.
6. Substitute $\lambda^i(w^i, \mathbf{p})$ into one of the other first-order conditions, $f_1^i(w^i, \mathbf{p})\mu_j^i + f_2^i(w^i, \mathbf{p})S_j^i(w^i, \mathbf{p}) = \lambda^i p_j$, to obtain $w^i = w^i(\mathbf{p})$ only.
7. Substitute this expression for $w^i(\mathbf{p})$ alone into the expressions for $x_j^i(w^i, \mathbf{p})$ to obtain $x_j^i = x_j^i(\mathbf{p})$ only for $j = 1, \ldots, n$.
8. Sum $n - 1$ of these expressions for $x_j^i(\mathbf{p})$ to obtain $n - 1$ equations in the $n - 1$ relative prices.
9. Solve the equations for the relative prices that produce market clearing. Denote these by $\mathbf{q}^* = (q_1^*, \ldots, q_{n-1}^*)$ to indicate that these prices clear all markets.
10. Substitute the optimal relative prices into the expressions for $x_j^i$ as a function of prices. This will give the number of shares of security $j$ held by individual $i$ at market equilibrium.

When both prices and security holdings have been expressed in terms of known parameters, the optimal solution is obtained.

**7.3.3. The Slope of the Efficient Frontier.** It has been shown in Theorem 7.1 that personal equilibrium implies that the rate of substitution of risk for return is constant. The slope of the efficient frontier is given by

$$\beta \equiv \frac{d\sigma}{d\rho} = \frac{\sigma}{\rho - r_n} = \frac{\sigma_r}{r - r_n} = \frac{(\mathbf{h}' \cdot \Sigma \cdot \mathbf{h})^{1/2}}{\mathbf{m}' \cdot \mathbf{h}} \tag{7.31}$$

This equation has been written to show that $\beta$ is a function of the vector $\mathbf{h}$. The solution for $\mathbf{h}$ implied by personal equilibrium is given by Equation 7.18.

This equation can be used to obtain an explicit solution for the slope of the market line.

THEOREM 7.3. The slope of the efficient frontier in the Sharpe model is given by

$$\beta(\mathbf{m}) = [\mathbf{m}' \cdot \Sigma^{-1} \cdot \mathbf{m}]^{-1/2} \tag{7.32}$$

PROOF. Substituting into Equation 7.31 for $\mathbf{h}$ from Equation 7.18 gives

$$\beta = \frac{(\mathbf{h}' \cdot \Sigma \cdot \mathbf{h})^{1/2}}{\mathbf{m}' \cdot \mathbf{h}} = \frac{(\mathbf{m}' \cdot (\Sigma')^{-1} \cdot \Sigma \cdot \Sigma^{-1} \cdot \mathbf{m})^{1/2}}{\mathbf{m}' \cdot \Sigma^{-1} \cdot \mathbf{m}}$$

$$= (\mathbf{m}' \cdot \Sigma^{-1} \cdot \mathbf{m})^{-1/2}$$

Q.E.D.

Equation 7.32 expresses $\beta$ as an explicit function of the vector of risk premiums. The vector $\mathbf{m}$ depends on absolute prices; however, this particular expression for $\beta$ is such that it depends only on relative prices.

COROLLARY 7.3.1. The variable $\beta$ depends only on relative prices and is given by

$$\beta(\mathbf{q}) = [(\mathbf{\mu} - \mu_n \mathbf{q})' \cdot \mathbf{S}^{-1} \cdot (\mathbf{\mu} - \mu_n \mathbf{q})]^{-1/2} \tag{7.33}$$

where $\mathbf{S}^{-1}$ is the inverse of $\mathbf{S}$.

PROOF. From Equation 7.32, we have

$$\beta = (\mathbf{m}' \cdot \Sigma^{-1} \cdot \mathbf{m})^{-1/2} = (\sum_\alpha \sum_\beta \sigma_{\alpha\beta}^{-1} m_\alpha m_\beta)^{-1/2}.$$

By definition of $m_\alpha$, $m_\beta$, and $\sigma_{\alpha\beta}^{-1}$, we have[19]

$$\begin{cases} m_\alpha = r_\alpha - r_n = p_\alpha^{-1}(\mu_\alpha - \mu_n q_\alpha) \\ m_\beta = r_\beta - r_n = p_\beta^{-1}(\mu_\beta - \mu_n q_\beta), \\ \sigma_{\alpha\beta}^{-1} = S_{\alpha\beta}^{-1} p_\alpha p_\beta \end{cases}$$

where $\sigma_{\alpha\beta}^{-1}$ is an element of $\Sigma^{-1}$ and $S_{\alpha\beta}^{-1}$ is the corresponding element of $\mathbf{S}^{-1}$;

$$\therefore \quad \sigma_{\alpha\beta}^{-1} m_\alpha m_\beta = S_{\alpha\beta}^{-1}(\mu_\alpha - \mu_n q_\alpha)(\mu_\beta - \mu_n q_\beta)$$

$$\Rightarrow \sum_\alpha \sum_\beta \sigma_{\alpha\beta}^{-1} m_\alpha m_\beta = (\mathbf{\mu} - \mu_n \mathbf{q})' \cdot \mathbf{S}^{-1} \cdot (\mathbf{\mu} - \mu_n \mathbf{q})$$

$$\Rightarrow \beta = [(\mathbf{\mu} - \mu_n \mathbf{q})' \cdot \mathbf{S}^{-1} \cdot (\mathbf{\mu} - \mu_n \mathbf{q})]^{-1/2}$$

Q.E.D.

[19] If $\mathbf{A} = [a_{ij}]$ and $\mathbf{B} = [b_{ij}]$ and $a_{ij} = \dfrac{b_{ij}}{c_i c_j}$, then $a_{ij}^{-1} = b_{ij}^{-1} c_i c_j$, where $a_{ij}^{-1}$ and $b_{ij}^{-1}$ are corresponding elements of $\mathbf{A}^{-1}$ and $\mathbf{B}^{-1}$.

The derivation of the expressions for $\beta$ given by Equations 7.32 and 7.33 required the use of only the conditions for personal equilibrium. It did not involve the use of the market-clearing equations. Hence, these expressions describe the slope of the relation between risk and return that an individual demands for his personal equilibrium, given any set of prices. Therefore $\beta$ will be the slope of the market line at market equilibrium only when the relative prices in the expression for $\beta$ are the prices which clear all markets.[20]

**7.3.4. The Role of the Utility Function.** We are now in a position to interpret the role of an individual's utility function in the determination of the slope of the capital-market line at equilibrium.

According to the Sharpe model, once the optimal portfolio of risky assets has been determined, an individual consults his utility function to determine what amount of wealth will be invested in this portfolio of risky assets, the market portfolio. In this approach, the utility function enters only in determining the scale of investment in risky assets; it does not enter into the determination of the optimal portfolio of risky assets or the slope of the line.

From our viewpoint of the reformulated Sharpe model, we see that the utility function becomes involved in the determination of those prices that produce market clearing and, thereby, determines that slope that corresponds to the so-called market portfolio. This is a crucial point: *The slope which corresponds to capital-market equilibrium depends on prices which in turn depend on the utility functions of the individuals in the market.* Thus, unless prices are such that all markets are cleared, the approach of first determining first the optimal portfolio of risky assets and then the scale of investment in these risky assets is incomplete. One cannot specify what the optimal portfolio will be, i.e., what the slope that corresponds to equilibrium will be, until one has specified the prices; and this specification of prices requires explicit consideration of utility functions.

**7.4. The Lintner Model of Capital-Market Equilibrium**

Lintner, like Sharpe, assumes: (1) Markets are perfect (no taxes, no transaction costs, short sales are allowed, shares are completely divisible, etc.). (2) All investors share the same one-period time horizon. (3) There exists a universally riskless asset with a fixed rate of return and no limit on borrowing. (4) Investors are in complete agreement about expected return and covariance of return.[21] (5) Differences in investor preferences are manifested by the form of their

---

[20] The concern with the market relation between risk and return in the Sharpe–Lintner–Mossin models resulted in a failure to emphasize that the equations being derived were primarily *personal*-equilibrium expressions that would be valid market-equilibrium expressions only if prices were such that markets were cleared.

[21] Lintner does relax the assumption of complete agreement at times.

utility function; however, all investors have only expected return $\rho$ and its standard deviation $\sigma$, as arguments of the utility function.

Lintner focuses his attention on the derivation of expected return in terms of given parameters. His concern is to find the relation between return and risk. According to the Lintner model, the optimal portfolio for an investor can be determined as follows: (1) The gross amount of wealth available for investment is specified. (2) The relative investment in risky assets is determined by maximizing the quantity $\theta$ defined as[22]

$$\theta \equiv \frac{r - r_n}{\sigma_r}, \tag{7.34}$$

where $r$ is the return on the portfolio of risky assets and $\sigma_r$ is its standard deviation. (3) The investment in the riskless asset is specified.

Equation 7.34 is derived as follows:[23]

$$\rho = (1 - w)r_n + wr = r_n + w(r - r_n) \tag{7.35}$$

$$\therefore \quad \rho = r_n + \frac{\sigma}{\sigma_r}(r - r_n), \quad \text{since } \sigma = w\sigma_r. \tag{7.36}$$

Letting $\theta$ be the coefficient of $\sigma$ in the expression above gives

$$\rho = r_n + \theta\sigma \quad \text{where } \theta \equiv \frac{r - r_n}{\sigma_r} = \frac{\rho - r_n}{\sigma}. \tag{7.37}$$

The maximization of $\theta$ and the attainment of equilibrium can be given a graphical interpretation in the $(\rho, \sigma)$ plane. If Equation 7.34 is written as

$$\sigma = \theta^{-1}(\rho - r_n),$$

$\theta$ is recognized as the reciprocal of the slope of a line in the $(\rho, \sigma)$ plane. Maximizing $\theta$ is equivalent to minimizing the slope of the line. The available investment opportunities, indicated by the curve IL in Figure 7.2, impose a limit on the extent to which the slope can be reduced. Given the investment opportunity locus IL, line 1 is the smallest possible slope; line 0 cannot be attained. The maximum attainable value of $\theta$ is the value that produces a line that is tangent to the investment opportunity locus IL. This graphical interpretation suggests the original graphical formulation of the Sharpe model.[24]

[22] Both $\theta$ and $w$ (the relative investment in risky assets) are functions of prices. The maximization of $\theta$, which is conditional on a given set of prices, determines personal equilibrium for an investor.
[23] This derivation is analogous to the one given by Lintner [15] in developing the expression for his objective function $\theta$.

[24] As already mentioned earlier in this chapter, Fama [6] has shown that the two models agree on a major result, their expression for the risk premium. The issue of the relation between the Sharpe and Lintner models will be treated in detail in Section 7.5 of this chapter.

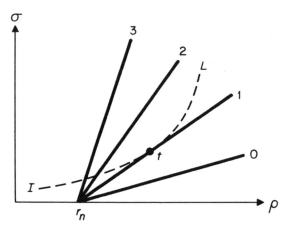

Fig. 7.2. The Lintner efficient frontier.

**7.4.1. Equilibrium Conditions and Properties.** THEOREM 7.4. At equilibrium in the Lintner model,

$$\frac{d\rho}{d\sigma} = \frac{\rho - r_n}{\sigma} = \frac{r_j - r_n}{\sigma_j} = \text{const} \quad j = 1, \ldots, n - 1 \tag{7.38}$$

$$\frac{r_j - r_n}{\sigma_j} = \frac{r_k - r_n}{\sigma_k} \quad j, k = 1, \ldots, n - 1 \tag{7.39}$$

PROOF.

1. The first-order conditions for maximization are

$$0 = \frac{d\theta}{dy_j} = \frac{(r_j - r_n)\sigma - (\rho - r_n)\sigma_j}{\sigma^2} \quad \text{where } \sigma_j \equiv \frac{d\sigma}{dy_j}$$

$$\Rightarrow (r_j - r_n)\sigma - (\rho - r)\sigma_j = 0 \text{ if } \sigma \neq 0 \tag{7.40}$$

$$\Rightarrow \frac{r_j - r_n}{\sigma_j} = \frac{\rho - r_n}{\sigma}. \tag{7.41}$$

This is part of the desired result.

2. To show $\dfrac{d\rho}{d\sigma} = \dfrac{\rho - r_n}{\sigma}$:

$$\rho = \sum_{j=1}^{n} r_j y_j$$

$$\Rightarrow d\rho = \sum_{j=1}^{n} r_j \, dy_j = \sum_{j=1}^{n} (r_j - r_n) \, dy_j,$$

since

$$\sum_{j=1}^{n} y_j = 1 \Rightarrow \sum_{j=1}^{n} dy_j = 0.$$

Solving Equation 7.40 for $r_j - r_n$ and substituting into the equation for $d\rho$ give

$$d\rho = \sum_{j=1}^{n} \left( \frac{\rho - r_n}{\sigma} \right) \frac{d\sigma}{dy_j} dy_j = \frac{\rho - r_n}{\sigma} \sum_{j=1}^{n} \frac{d\sigma}{dy_j} dy_j = \frac{\rho - r_n}{\sigma} d\sigma$$

$$\therefore \quad \frac{d\rho}{d\sigma} = \frac{\rho - r_n}{\sigma}.$$

3. The solution to the preceding equation is

$$\rho - r_n = c\sigma$$

$$\Rightarrow \frac{\rho - r_n}{\sigma} = c, \text{ where } c \text{ is a constant.}$$

Summarizing the results of steps 1, 2, and 3, it has been shown that

$$\frac{r_j - r_n}{\sigma_j} = \frac{r - r_n}{\sigma} = \frac{d\rho}{d\sigma} = c,$$

which is Equation 7.38.

4. Observe that the left-hand side of Equation 7.41 is independent of the subscript. Thus, Equation 7.41 implies

$$\frac{r_j - r_n}{\sigma_j} = \frac{r_k - r_n}{\sigma_k} \quad \text{for every } j, k = 1, \ldots, n - 1.$$

And this is Equation 7.39.

Q.E.D.

Note that no use is made of the fact that $\sigma$ is homogeneous of degree 1 in the proof of Theorem 7.4; the role of homogeneity is, however, critical in the proof of the analogous result for the Sharpe model. (The reason that no reference to homogeneity is necessary in the Lintner model is discussed in Section 7.5.3.)

The derivations in Theorem 7.4 are different from those in Lintner's paper. The variables in this derivation are the relative wealth invested in securities,

$(y_1, \ldots, y_n)$, and not relative wealth invested in risky assets, $(h_1, \ldots, h_{n-1})$. No explicit use has been made of the separation theorem.[25]

**7.4.2. Derivation of Results Using $\theta = \theta(h_1, \ldots, h_{n-1})$ as Objective Function.** The preceding derivations of Equations 7.38 and 7.39 assumed that the objective function was expressed in terms of the relative wealth variables $(y_1, \ldots, y_n)$. Lintner's original derivation was in terms of relative investment in the portfolio of risky assets, $(h_1, \ldots, h_{n-1})$. The derivations are, however, equivalent, as is now shown.[26]

THEOREM 7.5. At equilibrium, maximization of $\theta = \theta(h_1, \ldots, h_{n-1}) \Rightarrow$

$$\frac{dr}{d\sigma_r} = \frac{r - r_n}{\sigma_r} = \frac{r_j - r_n}{d\sigma_r/dh_j} = \text{const.} \tag{7.42}$$

PROOF.

$$\theta = \frac{\sum_{j=1}^{n-1} (r_j - r_n)h_j}{\sigma_r}.$$

First-order conditions are

$$0 = \frac{d\theta}{dh_j} = \frac{(r_j - r_n)\sigma_r - (r - r_n)(d\sigma_r/dh_j)}{\sigma_r^2} \qquad j = 1, \ldots, n-1$$

$$\Rightarrow r_j - r_n = \frac{r - r_n}{\sigma_r}\frac{d\sigma_r}{dh_j} \quad \text{if } \sigma_r \neq 0 \qquad j = 1, \ldots, n-1 \tag{7.43}$$

[25] Lintner [15, p. 34] stressed that "The particular formulas derived in sections II–IV depend *inter-alia* on the *Separation Theorem* and each investor's consequent preference for the stock mix which maximizes $\theta$." That the separation theorem holds for this particular objective function arises from the fact that $\theta$ is independent of $y_n$. From Equation 7.3, we have

$$\theta = \frac{\rho - r_n}{\sigma} = \frac{\sum_{j=1}^{n} (r_j - r_n)y_j}{\left(\sum_{j=1}^{n-1}\sum_{k=1}^{n-1} \sigma_{jk}y_jy_k\right)^{1/2}} = \frac{\sum_{j=1}^{n-1} (r_j - r_n)y_j}{\left(\sum_{j=1}^{n-1}\sum_{k=1}^{n-1} \sigma_{jk}y_jy_k\right)^{1/2}}.$$

Therefore, $\theta$ is independent of $y_n$! Since $\theta$ is independent of $y_n = 1 - w$, it cannot depend on the value of $w$. The fact that $\theta$ does not depend on $y_n$ is reflected in the fact that the $n$th first-order condition is identically true, i.e.,

$$\frac{(r_n - r_n)\sigma - (\rho - r_n)\sigma_n}{\sigma} \equiv 0.$$

[26] Lintner [15] used the fact that $\theta(h_1, \ldots, h_{n-1}) \in H^0$ to justify ignoring the constraint $\sum_{j=1}^{n-1} h_i = 1$. However, to express the constraint in the form in which $\phi \in H^0$, one must explicitly use

$$\Rightarrow \frac{r_j - r_n}{d\sigma_r/dh_j} = \frac{r - r_n}{\sigma_r}. \tag{7.44}$$

The total differential $dr$ is

$$dr = \sum_{j=1}^{n-1} r_j \, dh_j = \sum_{j=1}^{n-1} (r_j - r_n) \, dh_j \quad \text{since} \sum_{j=1}^{n-1} dh_j = 0$$

$$= \sum_{j=1}^{n-1} \left( \frac{r - r_n}{\sigma_r} \right) \frac{d\sigma_r}{dh_j} \, dh_j \quad \text{by Equation 7.36}$$

$$= \left( \frac{r - r_n}{\sigma_r} \right) \sum_{j=1}^{n-1} \frac{d\sigma_r}{dh_j} \, dh_j = \left( \frac{r - r_n}{\sigma_r} \right) d\sigma_r$$

$$\Rightarrow \frac{dr}{d\sigma_r} = \frac{r - r_n}{\sigma_r} = \frac{r_j - r_n}{d\sigma_r/dh_j} \quad \text{using Equation 7.37.}$$

The solution to $dr/d\sigma_r = (r - r_n)/\sigma_r$ gives $dr/d\sigma_r$ constant.

Q.E.D.

Equation 7.42 is similar in form to Equation 7.38. The difference in results is that the variables in Equation 7.38 are $(y_1, \ldots, y_n)$, not $(h_1, \ldots, h_{n-1})$, and that Equation 7.38 involves $\sigma$ and not $\sigma_r$. However, they are equivalent equations.

This expression summarizes personal equilibrium in the Lintner model. It is the same as the summary equation for personal equilibrium in the Sharpe model. Therefore, those properties of personal equilibrium and of market equilibrium for the Sharpe model can also be derived for the Lintner model.

**7.4.3. Price Determination in the Lintner Model.** Unlike Sharpe, Lintner considers the determination of equilibrium prices. The Lintner formulation of price determination proceeds as follows. When there is complete agreement,

---

the constraint, since $\theta$ can be written as a homogeneous function only when the constraint

$\sum_{j=1}^{n-1} h_j = 1$ is used explicitly to rewrite the equation as

$$\phi = \frac{\sum_{j=1}^{n-1} r_j h_j - r_n \sum_{j=1}^{n-1} (r_j - r_n) h_j}{\sigma_r} = \frac{\sum_{j=1}^{n-1} (r_j - r_n) h_j}{\sigma_r}.$$

the relative investment in risky assets must be the same as their relative market value,[27] i.e.,

$$h_j = \frac{q_j X_j}{\sum\limits_{\alpha=1}^{n-1} q_\alpha X_\alpha}. \tag{7.45}$$

This is a set of $n - 1$ equations in the $n - 1$ relative prices; however, it cannot be used to determine equilibrium prices, as Lintner suggests, because the set of equations is not independent.[28] That the equations are not independent is not surprising—they are derived from the definition of the variables involved, and the addition of the market-clearing requirement is not sufficient additional information. The crux of the problem is that prices cannot be determined without reference to the utility functions of the individuals and using Equation 7.45 to specify prices is an attempt to avoid this dependence of prices on the utility function (see Section 7.3.2, "The Complete Solution of the Sharpe Model").

**7.4.4. Relation of Results to Those of Lintner.** Theorems 7.4 and 7.5 summarize personal equilibrium in the Lintner model. The Lintner expression for the risk premium is given by[29]

$$r_j - r_n = \frac{r - r_n}{\sigma_r^2} \sum_{\alpha=1}^{n-1} \sigma_{j\alpha} h_\alpha = \lambda \sum_{\alpha=1}^{n-1} \sigma_{j\alpha} h_\alpha, \tag{7.46}$$

[27] To derive this expression, use Equation 7.27″ in Footnote 17, which gives

$$h_j^i = \frac{q_j x_j^i}{\sum\limits_{\alpha=1}^{n-1} q_\alpha x_\alpha^i}.$$

Then complete agreement and the method of ratio addition gives

$$h_j = \frac{q_j \sum\limits_{i=1}^{m} x_j^i}{\sum\limits_{i=1}^{m} \sum\limits_{\alpha=1}^{n-1} q_\alpha x_\alpha^i} = \frac{q_j X_j}{\sum\limits_{\alpha=1}^{n-1} q_\alpha X_\alpha}.$$

This expression is Equation 26a in the section of Lintner [15] entitled "Market Prices of Shares Implied by Shareholder Optimization in Purely Competitive Markets Under Idealized Uncertainty."

[28] To see that the equations are dependent, simply sum Equation 7.45 over $j$, giving

$$\sum_{j=1}^{n-1} h_j = \frac{\sum\limits_{\alpha=1}^{n-1} p_j X_j}{\sum\limits_{\alpha=1}^{n-1} p_\alpha X_\alpha} = 1.$$

[29] Equation 7.46 is Equation 12 of Lintner [15, p. 21].

where $\lambda \equiv (r - r_n)/\sigma_r^2$ is a parameter defined by Lintner. Since Equation 7.38 of Theorem 7.4 is the same as the summary equation of the Sharpe model, the derivation of the expression for $r_j - r_n$ given in Equation 7.46 is the same as the derivation of the expression for $r_j - r_n$ given in Corollary 7.1.1.

The measure of security risk implied by Equation 7.46 has the structure

$$\Delta(\text{return}) = \frac{d(\text{return})}{d(\text{risk})} \cdot (\text{security risk}).$$

Although the observation that excess returns are "linear in their own variance and pooled covariance" (Lintner [15, p. 21]) is correct, it obscures the marginal interpretation of risk.

The fact that Equations 7.38 and 7.39 are the same as Equations 7.11 and 7.12, the summary equations for the Sharpe model, means that results already derived in using these equations are valid for the Lintner model. To summarize the more significant of these results, it follows that

1. $h = \dfrac{\Sigma^{-1} \cdot m}{1' \cdot \Sigma^{-1} \cdot m}$

2. Corollaries 7.2.1, 7.2.2, and 7.2.3 hold.

3. $\theta = (m' \cdot \Sigma \cdot m)^{1/2} = [(\mu - \mu_n q) \cdot S^{-1} \cdot (\mu - \mu_n q)]^{1/2}$

### 7.5. Relation between the Sharpe and Lintner Models

How the Sharpe and Lintner models of capital-market equilibrium are related has been the subject of controversy. In his paper, Lintner [16] claimed to disagree with Sharpe and to have the more general model; Sharpe [27] in his reply agreed that there were differences and that Lintner's work superceded his own. This issue was recently revived by Fama [6].

Fama showed that the main result of the Lintner model (Equations 7.8 and 7.9 in this book) could be derived from the equilibrium requirements of the Sharpe model. Fama [6, p. 29] asserted that "there is no conflict between the Sharpe–Lintner models. Properly interpreted they lead to the same measure of the risk of an individual asset and to the same relationship between an asset's risk and its one-period expected return. The apparent conflicts discussed by Sharpe and Lintner are caused by Sharpe's concentration on a special stochastic process for describing returns that is not necessarily implied by his asset pricing model. When applied to the more general stochastic processes that Lintner treats, Sharpe's model leads directly to Lintner's conclusions."

As stated previously, the Sharpe model (properly interpreted) and the Lintner model have the same description of personal equilibrium. This result extends the work of Fama in showing that Lintner and Sharpe agree on the expression for the risk premium.

Since Sharpe and Lintner make essentially the same assumptions, differing only in the means by which they generate the efficient frontier, the possibility of equivalent models arises. The agreement established so far is necessary, but not sufficient, for equivalence. The possible relationships of these models are (1) They are equivalent. (2) One model is a special case of the other. (3) They are not equivalent or special cases of each other, but simply happen to agree.

**7.5.1. The Original Sharpe Model.** The generation of the efficient frontier in the Sharpe formulation is based on a Markowitz portfolio selection procedure. Let us formalize the procedure and maximize a Markowitz objective function, $\rho - c\Psi$, subject to a wealth constraint. Then we have as first-order conditions:

$$r_j - c\Psi_j = \lambda \quad j = 1, \ldots, n - 1$$

$$r_n = \lambda$$

$$\Rightarrow r_j - r_n = c\Psi_j$$

$$\Rightarrow \rho - r_n = c \sum_{j=1}^{n-1} \Psi_j y_j.$$

This will give a linear efficient frontier only if $\Psi$ is a homogeneous measure of risk.[30] When $\Psi = \sigma$, we have for the efficient frontier

$$\rho - r_n = c\sigma.$$

**7.5.2. The Two-Parameter Version of the Sharpe Model.** When the Sharpe model was presented as a special case of the two-parameter functional representation, the linearity of the efficient frontier arose from the solution of the differential equation giving the rate of substitution of risk for return. Crucial to the ability to solve this equation was the existence of a riskless asset and the homogeneity of the standard deviation.

The generation of the efficient frontier in the original (i.e., Markowitz-like) Sharpe model can be viewed as a special case of the two-parameter functional representation in which $f(\rho, \sigma) = \rho - c\sigma$. Then,

$$f_1 = 1$$

$$f_2 = -c$$

$$-\frac{f_1}{f_2} = c = \frac{\sigma}{\rho - r_n} \quad \text{from Theorem 7.1}$$

$$\Rightarrow \rho - r_n = c\sigma \quad \text{is the efficient frontier.}$$

[30] The essential role of homogeneity was not clear in Sharpe's argument.

**7.5.3. The Efficient Frontier in the Lintner Model.** The generation of the efficient frontier in the Lintner model arose from maximizing the Lintner objective function $\theta = (r - r_n)/\sigma_r$. The distinction between the Lintner model and the two previous cases is that the homogeneity of $\sigma$ was not used and was not necessary to obtain the linear efficient frontier—the linearity arose solely from the use of a ratio-type objective function.

To see clearly that the first-order conditions for a ratio objective function implies linearity between the numerator and denominator, let

$$R = \frac{g_1(y_1, \ldots, y_n)}{g_2(y_1, \ldots, y_n)},$$

where $g_1(y_1, \ldots, y_n)$ and $g_2(y_1, \ldots, y_n)$ are any two continuous functions and $g_2 \neq 0$. First-order conditions are

$$0 = \frac{g_2(dg_1/dy_j) - g_1(dg_2/dy_j)}{(g_2)^2} \qquad j = 1, \ldots, n$$

$$\Rightarrow \frac{dg_1}{dy_j} = \frac{g_1}{g_2} \frac{dg_2}{dy_j} \qquad j = 1, \ldots, n$$

$$\therefore \quad dg_1 = \sum_{j=1}^{n} \frac{dg_1}{dy_j} dy_j = \frac{g_1}{g_2} \sum_{j=1}^{n} \left(\frac{dg_2}{dy_j}\right) dy_j = \left(\frac{g_1}{g_2}\right) dg_2$$

$$\Rightarrow \frac{dg_1}{dg_2} = \frac{g_1}{g_2}.$$

The values of $g_1$ and $g_2$ consistent with this differential equation are $g_1 = cg_2$ where $c$ is a constant. Thus, we have a "linear frontier" relating $g_1$ and $g_2$. *Neither homogeneity nor a riskless asset were required for this result.*

Thus the mechanism by which the Lintner objective function generates the efficient frontier is somewhat different from the previous two cases, since each depends on homogeneity and a riskless asset to establish linearity. Although the Lintner objective function is so specialized that linearity of the efficient frontier is easily established, it is also a special case of the two-parameter representation $f(\rho, \Psi)$.

**7.5.4. Model Relationships.** How one views the relationship of the Sharpe and Lintner model depends on whether one refers to the original graphic formulation of Sharpe or the reformulation of the model as presented in this chapter.

Restricting Sharpe to the graphic formulation, we see that both Sharpe and Lintner presented special cases of the two-parameter functional representation. Since their objective functions are different special versions of $f(\rho, \sigma)$, Sharpe and Lintner have presented different models that generate a linear efficient frontier with the same expression for the slope.

On the other hand, if one means by the Sharpe model the reformation of Sharpe's work contained in this chapter (especially Theorem 7.1), then Lintner's generation of the efficient frontier is the special case in terms of the form of the objective function.[31]

**7.5.5. The Reason for Agreement.** We are now in a position to establish the source of the agreement that has been discovered between the Sharpe and the Lintner models. All agreement (as summarized in Equations 7.11 and 7.38) is a property of the rate of substitution of return for risk $d\rho/d\sigma$. For a two-parameter model, $f(\rho, \sigma)$, the rate of substitution is given by

$$\frac{d\rho}{d\sigma} = -\frac{f_2}{f_1} = \frac{\rho - r_n}{\sigma}.$$

*This result is clearly independent of the form of the function f.* Hence it will be the same for any model belonging to the class of mean-standard deviation models. Thus, the reason that Sharpe and Lintner agree on the result Fama obtained and on all properties of personal equilibrium derived in this chapter is that these results do not depend on the form of the function $f$.

The Mossin solution will also agree on these same results, since $F(\rho, \sigma^2) = f(\rho, \sigma)$ for some function $f$ (see Theorem 8.2 and the comments following the proof).

---

[31] In the body of his paper, Lintner [15] uses as his objective function $\theta = (r - r_n)/\sigma_r$. In the Appendix Lintner [15, p. 35] claims to show that the maximization of $\theta$ is equivalent to maximization of a general utility function $U(\rho, \sigma)$. However, the Lintner proof is not valid as shown in the following analysis.

Lintner's proof proceeds as follows: (1) Variables are changed from $(\rho, \sigma)$ to $(w, \sigma_r)$. (2) First-order conditions for maximization of $U(w, \sigma_r)$ are obtained. (3) These first-order conditions are shown to be equivalent to the first-order conditions for maximization of $\theta$.

The problem arises from the variable transformation in step 1 above. Writing out the transformation gives $\rho = wf(\sigma_r) + (1 - w)r_n$ and $\sigma = w\sigma_r$, where $r$ has been replaced by $f(\sigma_r)$ in the expression for $\rho$. This transformation will be valid if and only if the Jacobian of the transformation is non-zero. Computing the Jacobian $J$ gives $J = w[f(\sigma_r) - r_n - f'(\sigma_r)\sigma_r]$. When $J = 0$, we have $f'(\sigma_r) = [f(\sigma_r) - r_n]/\sigma_r$. But this is precisely the first-order condition required for maximization of $\theta$; hence, the condition for maximizing $\theta$ is the condition under which the transformation used in Lintner's proof is invalid, and the maximization of $\theta$ is not equivalent to maximization of a general utility function.

# 8
## The Mossin
## Formulation

The Mossin formulation of asset choice and market equilibrium is the most quantitative in the series of papers that have treated the subject. Mossin uses wealth and its variance as parameters of the utility function rather than return as its variance or standard deviation. Mossin uses shares as variables rather than relative wealth invested in securities. Thus he is able to treat prices explicitly; the effect of price changes on initial wealth and on security holdings is not hidden in the variables, as it is when one uses relative wealth.

Mossin makes the same assumptions as Sharpe and Lintner. The only difference in the assumptions is the use of variance instead of standard deviation as the argument of the objective function. He attempts to maximize $f(\overline{W}, V)$, where $V$ is the variance of $\tilde{W}$. He also explicitly treats the problem of market clearing rather than leaving it implicit in the model.

In Chapter 8 we first derive the Mossin results as a special case of the TPFR, present a general summarizing equation, determine expressions for the risk premium and measures of security risk, establish the equivalence between the Mossin and Sharpe-Lintner solutions for the relative portfolio of risky assets, and finally study in considerable depth the properties of the portfolio of risky assets. Particular attention is paid to the role of the assumptions and the distinction between personal and market equilibrium.

In studying the Mossin model we shall at times, in the latter part of the chapter, amend Mossin's work or reinterpret it in the light of the work of Sharpe, Lintner, or extensions to the mean-variance model achieved in Chapter 7. This critical and detailed review should not be construed as detracting from Mossin's paper, which this author regards as a significant and important contribution; because of its importance, he feels that it should be carefully studied and understood by all students of capital asset pricing models.

### 8.1. Personal Equilibrium in the Mossin Model

**8.1.1. The Rate of Substitution of Risk for Return.** The expression for the rate of substitution of risk for return in the Mossin model can be obtained by specializing the two-parameter functional representation. Theorem 5.4 gave the rate of substitution of risk for return when there exists a riskless asset. The general result is

$$\frac{d\psi^i}{dW^i} = \frac{\psi^i_j}{p_j m^i_j} = \frac{\psi^i_j}{\mu^i_j - \mu^i_j(p_j/p_n)}. \tag{8.1}$$

When the general measure of risk $\psi$ is replaced by variance, the Mossin measure of risk, this equation becomes

$$\frac{dV^i}{dW^i} = \frac{V^i_j}{p_j m^i_j} = \frac{2 \sum_{\alpha=1}^{n-1} S^i_{j\alpha} x^i_\alpha}{u^i_j - \mu^i_n(p_j/p_n)} \tag{8.2}$$

where $V^i_j = \dfrac{dV^i}{dx^i_j}$ and $S_{j\alpha} = \text{cov}\,(\mu_j, \mu_\alpha)$.

When complete agreement is assumed in the Mossin model, this equation becomes

$$\frac{dV^i}{dW^i} = \frac{2 \sum_{\alpha=1}^{n-1} S_{j\alpha} x^i_\alpha}{\mu_j - \mu_n(p_j/p_n)}, \tag{8.3}$$

since complete agreement in the Mossin model means that investors agree on the expected future price and its covariance with all securities, i.e., $\mu^i_j$ is equal to $\mu_j$ and $S^i_{j\alpha}$ is equal to $S_{j\alpha}$ for every $i$.

We have obtained Equation 8.3 by specializing the general two-parameter functional representation to the case in which (1) variance is the measure of risk; (2) there exists a riskless asset; and (3) investors are in complete agreement about expected future security prices and their covariance. This equation is also the result that Mossin obtains by maximizing the utility function of a given individual subject to a wealth constraint.[1] *Observe that this expression is a description of personal equilibrium.* It arises simply from maximizing an individual's utility function subject to a wealth constraint and does not necessarily require that market clearing occur.

Before proceeding with the development of the Mossin results, we shall specialize the marginal interpretation of an individual's asset choice to the Mossin model. Recall that in the general model an individual chooses his asset in such a manner that the ratio of marginal risk per dollar to the security risk premium is the same for all risky securities that he holds in his portfolio when there exists a riskless asset. In the Mossin model, where variance is the measure of risk, this interpretation becomes the following: The individual chooses his portfolio such that the ratio of marginal risk (the derivative of variance) to risk compensation is the same for all securities. This result follows directly from Equation 8.3 since the left-hand side of this equation is independent of the subscript denoting the security. By equating the right-

[1] Cf. Equation 5 of Mossin [19, p. 772].

hand side of Equation 8.3 for two different securities, one obtains

$$\frac{2 \sum_{\alpha=1}^{n-1} S_{j\alpha} x_\alpha^i}{p_j m_j} = \frac{2 \sum_{\alpha=1}^{n-1} S_{k\alpha} x_\alpha^i}{p_k m_k}, \tag{8.4}$$

where $p_j m_j = \mu_j - \mu_n(p_j/p_n)$ is the "risk compensation" for security $j$ in dollars. Substituting explicitly for the derivative in Equation 8.4 one obtains

$$\frac{dV^i/dx_j^i}{p_j m_j} = \frac{dV^i/dx_k^i}{p_k m_k}, \tag{8.5}$$

which is the desired expression for the relationship between the ratio of marginal risk to risk compensation for different securities.

Mossin (19, p. 774, Equation 9) obtains this result in that he derives Equation 8.4 although he does not interpret the expression in the numerator as the derivative of the variance and consequently does not interpret the quantity as marginal risk.

**8.1.2. Summary Equations for Personal Equilibrium.** The equations for the rate of substitution of risk for return can be summarized by a relation similar to the summary relation of the Sharpe model given by Theorem 7.1.

THEOREM 8.1. The summary equations for personal equilibrium in the Mossin model are

$$\frac{dV^i}{dW^i} = \frac{V_j^i}{p_j(r_j - r_n)} = \frac{\sum_{j=1}^{n} V_j^i x_j^i}{W^i - (1 + r_n^i)V_0^i} = \frac{2V}{W^i - (1 + r_n^i)V_0^i} \tag{8.6}$$

$$\frac{V_j^i}{p_j(r_j - r_n)} = \frac{V_k^i}{p_k(r_k - r_n)}$$

where $V_j^i = \dfrac{dV^i}{dx_j^i}$

PROOF. 1. The first part of Equation 8.6 follows immediately from Equation 8.2, the second part from the use of ratio addition, and the third part from Euler's Theorem and the fact that $V \in H^2$.

2. The second equation is Equation 8.5.

**8.1.3. Properties of the Mean-Variance Formulation.** In this section we shall briefly use Equation 8.2 to ascertain the measure of security risk, to derive an expression for the risk premium, and to relate the Mossin solution to the mean-standard deviation formulations. Equation 8.2 can be rewritten as

$$p_j m_j^i = p_j(r_j^i - r_n^i) = \frac{dW^i}{dV^i} V_j^i.$$

This expression has the structure

$$\text{security risk premium} = \frac{d\,(\text{wealth})}{d\,(\text{risk})} \cdot \text{marginal risk}$$

Letting $v^i = V^i/V^i_0$ be the variance per dollar, we can transform the expression to relative variables. Then we have

$$r^i_j - r^i_n = \left(\frac{dW^i}{dV^i}\right)\left(\frac{V^i_j}{p_j}\right) = \left(\frac{d\rho}{dv^i}\right)v^i_j$$

since

$$\frac{dW^i}{dV^i} = \frac{d\rho}{dv^i} \quad \text{and} \quad \frac{1}{p_j}\left(\frac{dV^i_j}{x^i_j}\right) = \frac{dv^i}{dy^i_j} = v^i_j$$

by Lemmas 5.3 and 5.1 respectively.
This equation has the structure

$$\Delta\,(\text{return}) = \frac{d\,(\text{return})}{d\,(\text{risk})} \cdot (\text{security risk}),$$

where $v^i_j$, the marginal variance per dollar, has been interpreted as security risk. This expression is a special case of the general result of the TPFR for the case in which variance is the risk measure and there is a riskless asset (cf. equation 5.20). The comparable expressions in the Sharpe or Lintner models are of the same structure, but they involve standard deviation as the risk measure. They are

$$r^i_j - r^i_n = \frac{d\rho^i}{d\sigma^i}\sigma^i_j.$$

THEOREM 8.2. The Mossin solution for the portfolio of risky assets is the same as the Sharpe-Lintner solution, even though Mossin uses variance and Sharpe and Lintner use standard deviation as the argument of their utility functions.

PROOF. The method of proof will be to show that the two expressions for the risk premium are the same. To accomplish this demonstration, we shall transform variance into standard deviation in the Mossin expression for the risk premium.

$$v = \sigma^2$$

$$\Rightarrow \frac{dv}{d\rho} = 2\sigma\frac{d\sigma}{d\rho}$$

and
$$\frac{dv}{dy} = 2\sigma \frac{d\sigma}{dy}.$$
Therefore, the Mossin expression for the risk premium becomes
$$r_j^i - r_n^i = \frac{d\rho^i}{dv^i}\left(\frac{dv^i}{dy_j^i}\right) = \frac{1}{2\sigma^i}\left(\frac{d\rho^i}{d\sigma^i}\right) \cdot 2\sigma^i\left(\frac{d\sigma^i}{dy_j^i}\right) = \left(\frac{d\rho^i}{d\sigma^i}\right)\sigma_j^i,$$
which is the desired result.

Q.E.D.

Mossin did not solve explicitly for an expression for the risk premium, nor did he show that equivalence of his solution to the mean-standard deviation formulations. However, for our purposes this result is significant—it means that the solution for **h** given by Theorem 7.2 and the properties of that solution are valid for the Mossin model. Moreover, it means that the expressions for the slope given in Theorem 7.3 and Corollary 7.3.1 are also valid. It also establishes the relation of the Mossin model to the Sharpe and Lintner models.

That the solution for **h**, the relative investment in risky assets, is the same whether one uses standard deviation or variance as the argument of the utility function is not surprising, because the solution for **h** is independent of the *form* of the function. Since $f(\rho, \sigma) = F(\rho, \sigma^2)$ for an appropriate choice of $F$, it is clear why the two solutions for **h** are equivalent. In general, any power of a risk measure will give the same solution for the security risk premium.

## 8.2. The Mossin Description of the Portfolio of Risky Assets

In the previous section we showed that the Mossin model has the same solution for the portfolio of risky assets as the reformulated Sharpe-Lintner model presented in Chapter 7. In this section we present the Mossin derivation of various properties of the portfolio, some alternative proofs, and some new results. The major focus is on the study of the market-equilibrium solution (as opposed to the personal-equilibrium solution) and the so-called "market properties" that the assumption of complete agreement enables one to derive. In the following analysis it is suggested that the reader pay particular attention to what results depend only on Equation 8.4 and what results also require the use of the market-clearing condition.

When the market-clearing condition is applied to Equation 8.4 by summing this equation over all $i$, one obtains
$$\frac{\sum_{i=1}^{m} \sum_{\alpha=1}^{n-1} S_{j\alpha} x_\alpha^i}{p_j m_j} = \frac{\sum_{i=1}^{m} \sum_{\alpha=1}^{n-1} S_{k\alpha} x_\alpha^i}{p_k m_k}.$$

When the order of summation is reversed and the market-clearing equation is employed, the expression above becomes

$$\frac{\sum\limits_{\alpha=1}^{n-1} S_{j\alpha}X_\alpha}{p_j m_j} = \frac{\sum\limits_{\alpha=1}^{n-1} S_{k\alpha}X_\alpha}{p_k m_k}. \tag{8.7}$$

Note that Equation 8.7 holds only at market equilibrium when all security markets are cleared, while Equation 8.4 is a personal-equilibrium result. Note also that complete agreement among all investors is required to obtain this expression. If complete agreement does not hold, then both the risk premium and the covariance depend on the investor, and Equation 8.4 must be replaced by Equation 8.3. When Equation 8.3 is summed over all investors, one obtains

$$\frac{1}{p_j}\sum_{i=1}^{m}\frac{\sum\limits_{\alpha=1}^{n-1} S_{j\alpha}^i x_\alpha^i}{m_j^i} = \frac{1}{p_k}\sum_{i=1}^{m}\frac{\sum\limits_{\alpha=1}^{n-1} S_{k\alpha}^i x_\alpha^i}{m_k^i}.$$

It is clear that this expression reduces to a simple form (such as Equation 8.7) only when there exists complete agreement. In general one does not have this nice type of expression in which one can meaningfully reverse the order of summation.

We now proceed with the development of the Mossin expression for the risk premium.

THEOREM 8.3 (*Mossin Result I*). "Risk premiums are such that the ratio between the total risk compensation paid for an asset and the variance of the total stock of the asset is the same for all assets" [19, p. 755], i.e.,

$$\frac{m_j(p_j X_j)}{V(j)} = \frac{m_k(p_k X_k)}{V(k)} \qquad j, k = 1, \ldots, n-1, \tag{8.8}$$

where

$p_j X_j \equiv$ market value of company $j$,

$m_j(p_j X_j) \equiv$ "total risk compensation" expected from asset $j$, \hfill (8.9)

$$V(j) \equiv X_j \sum_{\alpha=1}^{n-1} S_{j\alpha}X_\alpha = \text{"variance of the } total \text{ stock of asset } j\text{"}^2 \tag{8.10}$$

---

[2] Calling $V(j)$ a "variance" is somewhat of a misnomer. It is really the contribution of security $j$ to the variance of the market portfolio and not a variance per se.

PROOF. Multiply numerator and denominator of Equation 8.7 by $X_j$ on the left-hand side and $X_k$ on the right-hand side. This gives

$$\frac{X_j \sum_{\alpha=1}^{n-1} S_{j\alpha} X_\alpha}{m_j(p_j X_j)} = \frac{X_k \sum_{\alpha=1}^{n-1} S_{k\alpha} X_\alpha}{m_k(p_k X_k)}. \tag{8.11}$$

This expression is the reciprocal of Equation 8.8, the desired result, since

$$V(j) \equiv X_j \sum_{\alpha=1}^{n-1} S_{j\alpha} X_\alpha.$$

Q.E.D.

This result, summarized by Equation 8.8, is a valid market-equilibrium relationship. It can, however, be given a marginal interpretation in terms of the variance of the total stock of securities outstanding. Let

$$V(M) \equiv \sum_{\alpha=1}^{n-1} \sum_{\beta=1}^{n-1} S_{\alpha\beta} X_\alpha X_\beta = \text{``market variance,''} \text{ i.e., the variance of all securities outstanding} \tag{8.12}$$

DEFINITION 8.1. The *marginal risk of the market portfolio* with respect to a security is given by the derivative of the risk of the market portfolio with respect to the total outstanding stock of that security. Then

$$\frac{dV(M)}{dX_j} = 2 \sum_{\alpha=1}^{n-1} S_{j\alpha} X_\alpha. \tag{8.13}$$

Thus, Mossin's "variance of the total stock of an asset" is, for asset $j$,

$$V(j) = \frac{1}{2} X_j \frac{dV(M)}{dX_j} = X_j \sum_{\alpha=1}^{n-1} S_{j\alpha} X_\alpha.$$

It is seen that $V(j)$ is proportional to the marginal risk of the market portfolio with respect to security $j$, and that it is the contribution of security $j$ to market variance in the sense that $\sum_{j=1}^{n-1} V(j) = V(M)$.

The concept of the market portfolio and its marginal risk is meaningful only in the context of complete agreement among investors since the risk of the market portfolio is well-defined only when investors agree on the co-variance of securities.

We are now in a position to provide a marginal interpretation of Theorem 8.3.

COROLLARY 8.3.1. When there is complete agreement, the ratio of the marginal risk (marginal variance) of the market portfolio to dollar-risk premium is the same for all assets, i.e.,

$$\frac{\frac{dV(M)}{dX_j}}{p_j m_j} = \frac{\frac{dV(M)}{dX_k}}{p_k m_k} \qquad j, k = 1, \ldots, n - 1. \tag{8.14}$$

PROOF. Identifying $\sum_{k=2}^{n-1} S_{kj} X_j$ as $(1/2) \, dV(M)/dX_j$ in Equation 8.7 gives Equation 8.14 immediately.

Q.E.D.

This result depends critically upon complete agreement among investors concerning security parameters. It is valid only at market equilibrium; it requires that markets be cleared.

Corollary 8.3.1 is a direct generalization to the market portfolio of the marginal interpretation of personal equilibrium. The form of Equations 8.5 and 8.14 is the same! The reason that this generalization is possible and its critical dependence on complete agreement among investors is established in Theorem 8.4.

THEOREM 8.4. If investors are in complete agreement about security parameters, then at market equilibrium any individual's marginal risk with respect to security $j$ will be proportional to the marginal risk of the market portfolio with respect to security $j$, i.e.,

$$\frac{dV^i}{dx_j^i} = d^i \frac{dV(M)}{dX_j} \qquad j = 1, \ldots, n - 1, \tag{8.15}$$

where $d^i$ is a constant characteristic of individual $i$, but depends on the utility function of all individuals for the expression of its value.

PROOF. From Equation 8.5 we have

$$\frac{dV^i}{dx_j^i} = c^i(p_j m_j) \qquad \begin{array}{l} i = 1, \ldots, n \\ j = 1, \ldots, n - 1, \end{array} \tag{8.16}$$

where at equilibrium $c^i$ is a constant characteristic of individual $i$. Summing this equation over $i$ gives

$$\sum_{i=1}^{m} \frac{dV^i}{dx_j^i} = \left( \sum_{i=1}^{m} c^i \right) p_j m_j. \tag{8.17}$$

But

$$\sum_{i=1}^{m} \frac{dV^i}{dx_j^i} = \sum_{i=1}^{m} \left( 2 \sum_{\alpha=1}^{n-1} S_{j\alpha} x_\alpha^i \right) = 2 \sum_{\alpha=1}^{n-1} S_{j\alpha} X_\alpha = \frac{dV(M)}{dX_j}. \tag{8.18}$$

From Equations 8.17 and 8.18 we have

$$\frac{dV(M)}{dX_j} = \left( \sum_{i=1}^{n} c^i \right)(p_j m_j).$$  (8.19)

From Equations 8.16 and 8.19 we have

$$\frac{dV^i}{dx_j^i} = \frac{c^i}{\sum\limits_{i=1}^{m} c^i} \frac{dV(M)}{dX_j}.$$  (8.20)

Defining $d^i$ to be $c^i / \sum\limits_{i=1}^{m} c^i$, Equation 8.20 becomes 8.15, the desired result.

Q.E.D.

COROLLARY 8.4.1. The constants $c^i$ and $d^i$ are given by

$$c^i = \frac{2w^i}{\mathbf{1}' \cdot \Sigma^{-1} \cdot \mathbf{m}}$$  (8.21)

$$d^i = \frac{c^i}{\sum\limits_{i=1}^{m} c^i} = \frac{w^i}{\sum\limits_{i=1}^{m} w^i}$$  (8.22)

where $w^i = \sum\limits_{j=1}^{n-1} y_j^i$ is the fraction of wealth invested in risky securities, $\Sigma^{-1}$ is the inverse of the covariance matrix of returns, and $\mathbf{m}$ is the vector of security risk premiums.

PROOF. To derive Equation 8.21 we shall first rewrite Equation 8.16 to give an expression for the security risk premium, then use the fact that the Sharpe-Lintner expression is the same as the Mossin result, and, finally use the solution for $\mathbf{h}$ to evaluate $c^i$. Rewriting Equation 8.16 gives

$$m_j = \frac{1}{c^i} \frac{V_j^i}{p_j} = \frac{1}{c^i} v_j^i$$

$$\therefore \quad r_j - r_n = \frac{2}{c^i} \sum_{k=1}^{n-1} \sigma_{jk} y_k^i = \frac{2w^i}{c^i} \sum_{k=1}^{n-1} \sigma_{jk} h_k,$$

since $m_j = r_j - r_n$, and $v_j^i = 2 \sum\limits_{k=1}^{n-1} \sigma_{jk} y_k^i$, and $y_k^i = w^i h_k$. In Theorem 8.2 we showed that the Mossin expression for the security risk premium is the same as the Sharpe-Lintner-Fama expression for the security risk premium. From

Equation 7.8 we have

$$r_j - r_n = \frac{r - r_n}{\sigma_r^2} \sum_{k=1}^{n-1} \sigma_{jk} h_k$$

where, it is recalled, $r$ is the return on the portfolio of risky assets and $\sigma_r$ is its standard deviation.

Comparing these two expressions for $r_j - r_n$ gives

$$c^i = 2w^i \cdot \frac{\sigma_r^2}{r - r_n}.$$

Using the expression for $\mathbf{h}$ given by Equation 7.18 of Theorem 7.2 to evaluate $(r - r_n)/\sigma_r^2$ gives

$$\frac{r - r_n}{\sigma_r^2} = \frac{\mathbf{m}' \cdot \mathbf{h}}{\mathbf{h}' \cdot \Sigma \cdot \mathbf{h}} = \mathbf{1}' \cdot \Sigma^{-1} \cdot \mathbf{m}$$

after substituting for $\mathbf{h}$ and simplifying. Therefore,

$$c^i = \frac{2w^i}{\mathbf{1}' \cdot \Sigma^{-1} \cdot \mathbf{m}}$$

$$\Rightarrow d^i = \frac{c^i}{\displaystyle\sum_{i=1}^{m} c^i} = \frac{w^i}{\displaystyle\sum_{i=1}^{m} w^i}.$$

Q.E.D.

Clearly $c^i$ and $d^i$ depend on the relative amount of wealth invested in risky securities. Thus, $c^i$ depends on how much individual $i$ decides to borrow as well as the prices faced by individual $i$; $c^i$ is a personal equilibrium constant characteristic of individual $i$. The constant $d^i$ depends on how individual $i$ and all individuals in the market decide to borrow. It thus depends on the form of the utility function of all investors and is defined only at market equilibrium when there is complete agreement as well as a riskless asset.[3]

**8.2.1. Composition of Equilibrium Portfolios.** In Chapter 7 a number of properties of the portfolio of risky assets were developed. In order to study the relation between the Sharpe-Lintner results (as extended in Chapter 7) and the Mossin results, we shall present the Mossin derivation and alternative proofs. The purpose here is to analyze the structure of the arguments, to gain insight into the models, and to distinguish between personal and market

---

[3] Recall from the description of the market-equilibrium solution in Chapter 7 that the values of $w_j^i$ at market equilibrium depend upon the equilibrium prices and, therefore, on the utility functions of all individuals in the market.

equilibrium results; the reader who is primarily interested in answers rather than the method of analysis should refer to Section 7.3.

THEOREM 8.5 (*Mossin Result II*). "In equilibrium, prices must be such that each individual will hold the same percentage of the total outstanding stock of all risky assets" [19, p. 775], i.e.,

$$z_j^i = z_k^i = z^i \qquad \begin{matrix} i = 1, \ldots, m \\ j, k = 1, \ldots, n-1 \end{matrix} \tag{8.23}$$

where $z_j^i \equiv (x_j^i)/X_j$ is the fraction of the shares of security $j$ held by $i$.

MOSSIN PROOF. Dividing Equation 8.4 by Equation 8.7 we have

$$\frac{\sum\limits_{\alpha=1}^{n-1} S_{j\alpha} x_\alpha^i}{\sum\limits_{\alpha=1}^{n-1} S_{j\alpha} X_\alpha} = \frac{\sum\limits_{\alpha=1}^{n-1} S_{k\alpha} x_\alpha^i}{\sum\limits_{\alpha=1}^{n-1} S_{k\alpha} X_\alpha} \qquad j, k = 1, \ldots, n-1. \tag{8.24}$$

Define $b_{j\alpha}$ to be

$$b_{j\alpha} \equiv \frac{S_{j\alpha} X_\alpha}{\sum\limits_{\beta=1}^{n-1} S_{j\beta} X_\beta} \Rightarrow \sum\limits_{\alpha=1}^{n-1} b_{j\alpha} = 1. \tag{8.25}$$

Then Equation 8.24 can be rewritten as

$$\sum\limits_{\alpha=1}^{n-1} \left( \frac{S_{j\alpha} X_\alpha}{\sum\limits_{\beta=1}^{n-1} S_{j\beta} X_\beta} \right) z_\alpha^i = \sum\limits_{\alpha=1}^{n-1} \left( \frac{S_{j\alpha} X_\alpha}{\sum\limits_{\beta=1}^{n-1} S_{k\beta} X_\beta} \right) z_\alpha^i$$

$$\Rightarrow \sum\limits_{\alpha=1}^{n-1} b_{j\alpha} z_\alpha^i = \sum\limits_{\alpha=1}^{n-1} b_{k\alpha} z_\alpha^i \qquad j, k = 1, \ldots, n-1.$$

Let $a^i$ be the common value of these sums, i.e.,

$$\sum\limits_{\alpha=1}^{n-1} b_{j\alpha} z_\alpha^i = a^i \qquad j = 1, \ldots, n-1 \tag{8.26}$$

$$\Rightarrow z_j^i = a^i \sum\limits_{\alpha=1}^{n-1} b_{j\alpha}^{-1}, \tag{8.27}$$

where $b_{j\alpha}^{-1}$ is an element of the inverse of the matrix $B = [b_{j\alpha}]$.

Since $\sum\limits_{\alpha=1}^{n-1} b_{j\alpha} = 1$ for every $j$, we have that[4]

$$\sum_{\alpha=1}^{n-1} b_{j\alpha}^{-1} = 1$$

$\Rightarrow z_j^i = a^i$         from Equation 8.27

$\Rightarrow z_j^i = z_k^i = z^i$     for $j, k = 1, \ldots, n-1$.          (8.28)

Q.E.D.

The preceding proof of Mossin Result II is essentially that presented by Mossin [19, p. 775]. It employs Equation 8.7, a result which holds only at market equilibrium; therefore, the result is valid only when the market is in equilibrium. An alternative proof can be based on the fact that all individuals hold the same relative portfolio of risky assets.[5]

PROOF 2. $h_j = h_j^i = y_j^i w^i = \dfrac{p_j x_j^i w^i}{V_0^i}$     $\begin{array}{l} i = 1, \ldots, m \\ j = 1, \ldots, n-1 \end{array}$

$\Rightarrow \dfrac{h_j}{h_k} = \dfrac{p_j x_j^i}{p_k x_k^i}$

$\Rightarrow \dfrac{h_j}{h_k} = \dfrac{p_j \sum\limits_{i=1}^{m} x_j^i}{p_k \sum\limits_{i=1}^{m} x_k^i} = \dfrac{p_j X_j}{p_k X_k}$

$\Rightarrow \dfrac{x_j^i}{X_j} = \dfrac{x_k^i}{X_k}$

or

$z_j^i = z_k^i$     $i = 1, \ldots, m$   and   $j, k = 1, \ldots, n-1$.

Q.E.D.

[4] It can be shown that if matrix B is such that the sum of each row is one, then the inverse of B has the same property if $B^{-1}$ exists. To put Equation 8.26 into this framework, let B be the matrix of coefficients in 8.26. Then this equation can be rewritten as

$B \cdot z^i = a^i \mathbf{1}$

$\Rightarrow z^i = a^i B^{-1} \cdot \mathbf{1}$

$\Rightarrow z_j^i = a^i \sum\limits_{\alpha=1}^{n-1} b_{j\alpha}^{-1} = a^i$,    which is Equation 8.28.

[5] This proof is the same as that given in Chapter 7 to show that the Sharpe model implies that each individual holds the same percentage of the outstanding stock of all risky assets.

This proof depends only on the facts that (1) all individuals hold the same portfolio of risky assets; and (2) the market must be cleared in equilibrium. Proof 2 is more direct than the Mossin proof. It proceeds directly from the solution for the portfolio of risky assets and uses only the fact that this solution must be the same for every investor under complete agreement. Although Proof 2 is more direct, the result is the same. In fact, Mossin Result II can be used to show that investors hold the same relative portfolio of risky assets.

COROLLARY 8.5.1.

$$z_\alpha^i = z_\beta^i = z^i \qquad \text{for every } i = 1, \ldots, m \text{ and } \alpha, \beta = 1, \ldots, n-1$$

$$\Rightarrow h_\beta^i = h_\beta^j = h_\beta \qquad \text{for every } i, j = 1, \ldots, m \text{ and } \beta = 1, \ldots, n-1$$

PROOF. $z_\alpha^i = z_\beta^i$

$$\Rightarrow \frac{x_\alpha^i}{x_\beta^i} = \frac{X_\alpha}{X_\beta} \qquad\qquad\qquad\qquad\qquad\qquad (8.29)$$

$$\Rightarrow \frac{x_\alpha^i}{x_\beta^i} = \frac{x_\alpha^j}{x_\beta^j}$$

since the right-hand side of Equation 8.29 is independent of the superscript

$$\Rightarrow \frac{p_\alpha x_\alpha^i}{p_\beta x_\beta^i} = \frac{p_\alpha x_\alpha^j}{p_\beta x_\beta^j}$$

$$\Rightarrow \frac{p_\alpha x_\alpha^i w^i / V_0^i}{p_\beta x_\beta^i w^i / V_0^i} = \frac{p_\alpha x_\alpha^j w^j / V_0^j}{p_\beta x_\beta^j w^j / V_0^j}$$

$$\Rightarrow \frac{h_\alpha^i}{h_\beta^i} = \frac{h_\alpha^j}{h_\beta^j}$$

$$\Rightarrow h_\alpha^i = \left(\frac{h_\beta^i}{h_\beta^j}\right) h_\alpha^j.$$

And summing over $\alpha$, one has

$$\sum_{\alpha=1}^{n-1} h_\alpha^i = 1 = \frac{h_\beta^i}{h_\beta^j} \sum_{\alpha=1}^{n-1} h_\alpha^j = \frac{h_\beta^i}{h_\beta^j}$$

$$\Rightarrow h_\beta^i = h_\beta^j = h_\beta.$$

Q.E.D.

COROLLARY 8.5.2. $z_j^i = z_k^i = z^i$ at market equilibrium $\Leftrightarrow h_\alpha^i = h_\alpha^j = h_\alpha$ at market equilibrium.

PROOF. Follows directly from Proof 2 of Theorem 8.5 and Corollary 8.5.1.

Although the two results are equivalent *at market equilibrium*, the use of the solution of the equations of personal equilibrium shows that $h_\alpha^i = h_\alpha^j = h_\alpha$ under complete agreement (cf. Theorem 7.2, especially Equation 7.18). This is a property of personal equilibrium which, therefore, must also hold at market equilibrium. However, $z_j^i = z_k^i = z^i$ holds only at market equilibrium. The logical order of proof is to establish first the personal equilibrium result and then the market equilibrium result by using the market clearing equations. Since the fact that individuals hold the same portfolio of risky assets under complete agreement is primarily a personal equilibrium result, it is one reason to regard as more fundamental this result than the fact that the relative investment in risky assets is the same for all investors at market equilibrium.

THEOREM 8.6 (*Mossin Result III*). "The ratio between the holding of two risky assets is the same for all individuals" [19, p. 776], i.e.

$$\frac{x_\alpha^i}{x_\beta^i} = \frac{x_\alpha^j}{x_\beta^j}.$$

MOSSIN PROOF. $z_j^i = z_k^i = z^i \qquad i = 1, \ldots, m$

$$\Rightarrow \frac{z_\alpha^i}{z_\alpha^j} = \frac{z_\beta^i}{z_\beta^j}$$

$$\Rightarrow \frac{x_\alpha^i}{x_\alpha^j} = \frac{x_\beta^i}{x_\beta^j}$$

$$\Rightarrow \frac{x_\alpha^i}{x_\beta^i} = \frac{x_\alpha^j}{x_\beta^j}$$

Q.E.D.

This proof, once Result II is obtained, is easy and straightforward. It also follows from the fact that the relative investment in risky assets is the same for all investors under complete agreement. In fact, that the relative investment in two risky assets be the same is *all* that is required to prove Mossin Result III. This fact is established in the following alternative proof.

PROOF 2. $h_\alpha^i = h_\alpha^j = h_\alpha \quad$ or $\quad (p_\alpha x_\alpha^i) \frac{w^i}{V_0^i} = p_\alpha x_\alpha^j \frac{w^j}{V_0^j}$

$$\Rightarrow \frac{x_\alpha^i}{x_\alpha^j} = \frac{w^j}{w^i} \frac{V_0^i}{V_0^j} \qquad \alpha = 1, \ldots, n-1$$

$$\Rightarrow \frac{x_\alpha^i}{x_\alpha^j} = \frac{x_\beta^i}{x_\beta^j}.$$

Q.E.D.

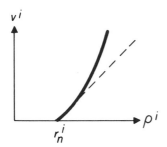
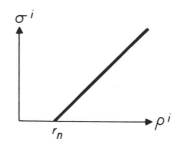

Fig. 8.1. $(\rho^i, v^i)$ and $(\rho^i, \sigma^i)$ curves.

Note that Proof 2 used a personal equilibrium result; hence, Mossin Result III is primarily a property of personal equilibrium. This fact is not clear in Proof 1 since it depends on Mossin Result II, which is valid only at market equilibrium. Thus, Proof 2 is more general than Proof 1, and Mossin Result III has more general validity than Proof 1 implies, since it holds at personal as well as market equilibrium.

### 8.3. The Efficient Locus

Let $v^i = V^i/V_0^i$ be the *variance per dollar* of individual $i$'s portfolio. In the Mossin model the measure of risk is variance, a function that is homogeneous of degree 2. We know from Chapter 5 that a closed-form solution exists. From Equation 5.43 we have

$$\rho^i - r_n = c^i\sqrt{v^i}, \tag{8.30}$$

where $v^i$ has replaced $\Psi^i$ and $r_n^i = r_n$ has been used. Equation 8.30 is clearly not linear in variance $v^i$! It is, however, linear in standard deviation per dollar, i.e.,

$$\rho^i - r_n = c^i\sigma^i, \tag{8.31}$$

as we would expect, since the Mossin and the Sharpe models have been shown to have the same solution for the portfolio of risky assets.

Note that if one speaks of a risk-return curve, then one speaks of a plot of $(\rho^i, v^i)$ combinations and the curve is not linear; if, however, one speaks of a square root of risk-return curve, then one is considering a $(\rho^i, \sigma^i)$ curve that is linear, as sketched in Figure 8.1.

This is an indication of the ambiguity of choice of the risk measure that arises in the TPFR. Even though the choice makes no difference in the solution, it does affect how one interprets the solution including whether one regards the efficient locus as linear! The slope of the $(\rho, \sigma)$ curve is given by Theorem 7.3 and Corollary 7.3.1. The efficient locus will be the same for all individuals with complete agreement and one can speak of a market curve.

# Appendix 1.
## One-Step Portfolio Selection—
## A Consideration of Information and Computation Requirements

The Markowitz portfolio selection procedure involves two steps once the data are provided. These are (1) generation of the efficient frontier; and (2) selection of the point on the efficient frontier that maximizes an investor's utility function. Thus considerable effort is expended in generating from the raw data the efficient frontier when a given investor will ultimately be concerned with only one point.

In this appendix a one-step portfolio-selection procedure is presented. This procedure determines only the optimal portfolio for an individual investor without generating an efficient frontier; it simply generates the point on the efficient frontier that would be chosen without generating the frontier. The method is classical optimization.

After the one-step procedure is developed, the information and computation requirements of the two methods are compared.

**1.1. The One-Step Procedure.** To keep the analysis within the Markowitz framework, assume that (1) an investor's utility function depends only on mean and variance, and (2) the utility function is continuous and differentiable.[1] Let the following notation be defined:

$y_j$ = relative investment in security $j$.

$r = \sum\limits_{j=1}^{n-1} r_j y_j$ is expected return.

$\sigma = \sum\limits_{i=1}^{n-1} \sum\limits_{j=1}^{n-1} \sigma_{ij} y_i y_j.$

There are $n - 1$ securities.

To maximize $U(r, \sigma)$ subject to a wealth constraint, form the Lagrangian $L$,

$$L = U(r, \sigma) - \lambda \left( \sum_{i=1}^{n-1} y_i - 1 \right).$$

---

[1] Strictly speaking, the Markowitz procedure requires only that $U(r, \sigma)$ be continuous so that one is ensured of a tangency point. However, I believe that one would find it difficult to present a meaningful utility function that is continuous but not differentiable.

First-order conditions for maximizing $L$ are

$$0 = \frac{\partial L}{\partial y_j} = \frac{\partial U}{\partial r} r_j + \left(\frac{\partial U}{\partial \sigma}\right) \frac{d\sigma}{dy_j} - \lambda \qquad j = 1. \ldots, n - 1$$

$$0 = \frac{\partial L}{\partial \lambda} = \sum_{j=1}^{n-1} y_j - 1.$$

These expressions are a set of $n$ equations in $n$ unknowns, the $n - 1$ $y_i$, and the Lagrange multiplier $\lambda$. If there is an optimal solution to the Markowitz portfolio problem, then there should also be a solution to the set of equations given here.

**1.2. Computational Requirements.** For most utility functions this set of equations is nonlinear and analytically untractable; however, by using numerical methods, they can be solved by a computer. The computational effort will depend on the algorithm used to solve the equations. It should be possible to develop special algorithms that take advantage of features of optimal portfolio solutions, such as the fact that in general only a few securities enter the portfolio. To provide an indication of how such an algorithm might proceed, consider the following suggestions. (1) Generate a good starting solution by solving a special subproblem such as a linear programing problem that picks, say, $k$ of the $n$ securities and sets all other $y_i = 0$. (2) Develop a choice procedure for trying various new candidates for entry, say, a rule such as choosing $y_i$ with a high ratio of return to variance and also a low correlation with the current trial portfolio.

The purpose of this appendix is not to develop an actual algorithm for one-step portfolio selection, but rather to indicate that the problem can be solved in such a fashion by solving a set of $n$ equations in $n$ unknowns by numerical methods. The purpose is to suggest that one-step solutions should be competitive with the two-step procedure of Markowitz and that the attractiveness of the Markowitz procedure is not primarily computational, but has to do with information requirements as discussed in 1.3.

**1.3. Information Requirements.** I believe that the reason for the prominence of Markowitz-like portfolio selection models is not its computational merit,[2] but rather the fact that reference to an individual's utility function is postponed until the latest possible time. Thus, generation of the efficient frontier allows (1) much of the search to be performed without reference to the utility function; (2) the same search to be performed for a number of different utility functions; and (3) selection of the optimal point without even explicitly specifying the mathematical form of the utility function.

[2] Recall that quadratic programing was a difficult task on the small, slow computers of the early 1950s.

The first two points are self-evident; the last one may not be, although it is the most significant. Once the efficient frontier has been specified, the optimal point can be specified by moving along the efficient frontier in the direction of increasing utility until one reaches a point at which utility no longer increases. This is the optimal point. For a risk-averse investor, the discovery of such a unique point is ensured. The significant aspect of this procedure is that it is never necessary to specify explicitly the mathematical form of the utility function. *Thus, not only is explicit reference to the utility function postponed until the latest possible moment, but the actual specification of the utility function is also circumvented.*

In contrast, the one-step procedure previously outlined requires the explicit specification of the form of the utility function at an early stage of the analysis. Hence the ability to specify accurately the form of the utility function is crucial to the one-step classical procedure, but not the two-step Markowitz procedure. Thus, the Markowitz model has effectively reduced the information requirements required for portfolio selection.

I believe that this feature of the Markowitz model has been neglected in the theoretical literature because an actual utility function is assumed to exist and a tangency point sketched in a graph depicting the efficient frontier and an isoutility curve.

It is not generally stressed in Markowitz portfolio selection that only the existence of $U(r, \sigma)$ is necessary; really knowing the form of $U(r, \sigma)$ is not crucial. In my opinion, it is the reduction in the information requirements that is the significant advantage of the Markowitz model over the one-step utility maximization procedure.[3] This feature is significant not only for the actual selection of portfolios, but also for research in the field of portfolio selection. However, attempts directly to generalize the two-step procedure of Markowitz to market equilibrium models cannot avoid the information requirements and are, moreover, analytically more complicated and less amenable to analysis than the one-step procedure.

---

[3] Other possible advantages are the ease with which sensitivity analysis can be performed and the amenability to approximation procedures such as the Sharpe diagonal model; however, the merits of these features depend on the form of the utility function and the type of algorithm employed in the one-step procedure. Another possible advantage is the ability to handle inequality constraints in the programming format. Such constraints would occur if short sales were prohibited. The analysis of this chapter can be generalized to compare again one-step versus two-step optimization in the case of inequality constraints.

**Appendix 2.
Derivation
of $M_k$ for a
Normal
Distribution**

Let $I_k \equiv \displaystyle\int_0^\infty z^k \exp(-z^2/2)\,dz$.

In order to evaluate $M_k$ as a function of variance $V$, it is necessary to establish a recursion relation for $I_k$.

LEMMA 1. For even $k$,

$$I_k = (k-1)I_{k-2} = \ldots = (k-1)!!\,I_2,$$

where

$$(k-1)!! \equiv (k-1)(k-3)\ldots 5\cdot 3\cdot 1.$$

PROOF. Integrating $I_k$ by parts, one has

$$I_k = -z^{k-1}\exp(-z^2/2)|_0^\infty + (k-1)\int_0^\infty z^{(k-2)}\exp(-z^2/2)\,dz$$

$$= (k-1)\,I_{k-2}$$

$$\vdots$$

$$= (k-1)!!\,I_2$$

Q.E.D.

LEMMA 2. For $k$ even, the $k$th central moment of a normal distribution $M_k$ is given by

$$M_k = (k-1)!!\sigma^k.$$

PROOF.

$$M_k \equiv \frac{1}{\sqrt{2\pi}\,\sigma}\int_{-\infty}^\infty (W-\overline{W})^k \exp[-(W-\overline{W})^2/2\sigma^2]\,dW$$

$$= \frac{\sigma^k}{\sqrt{2\pi}}\int_{-\infty}^\infty z^k \exp(-z^2/2)\,dz$$

$$= \sqrt{\frac{2}{\pi}}\,\sigma^k I_k \quad \text{by definition of } I_k$$

$$= \sqrt{\frac{2}{\pi}} \sigma^k (k-1)!! I_2 \quad \text{by Lemma 1}$$

$$= (k-1)!! \sigma^k \quad \text{since } I_2 = \sqrt{\frac{\pi}{2}}$$

Q.E.D.

LEMMA 3. For $k$ odd, $M_k = 0$ for a normal distribution.

PROOF. $M_k = \displaystyle\int_{-\infty}^{\infty} (W - \overline{W})^k f(W)\, dW$

Since $f(W)$ is symmetric about $\overline{W}$ for a normal distribution, and since $(W - \overline{W})^k$ is antisymmetric, the integrand is antisymmetric, and, therefore, $M_k = 0$ for $k$ odd.

Q.E.D.

# References

**Arrow, K. J.**    1. "The Role of Securities in the Optimal Allocation of Risk Bearing," *Review of Economic Studies*, **86** (1964).

——.    2. *Aspects of the Theory of Risk Bearing*. Helsinki: Yrjo Fahnsoon Foundation, 1965.

**Baumol, William J.**    3. "An Expected Gain-Confidence Limit Criterion for Portfolio Selection," *Management Science*, **10** (October 1963), 174–82.

**Diamond, P. A.**    4. "The Role of a Stock Market in a General Equilibrium Model with Technological Uncertainty," *American Economic Review*, **57**, 759–776.

**Fama, Eugene F.**    5. "Portfolio Analysis in a Stable Paretian Market," *Management Science*, January 1963, pp. 404–419.

——.    6. "Risk, Return and Equilibrium: Some Clarifying Comments," *Journal of Finance*, February 1968, pp. 29–40.

**Farrar, Donald E.**    7. *The Investment Decision Under Uncertainty*. Englewood Cliffs, N.J.: Prentice-Hall, 1962.

**Friedman, Milton, and L. J. Savage**    8. "The Utility Analysis of Choices Involving Risk," *Journal of Political Economy*, **56**, 4 (August 1948), 279–304.

**Graham, Benjamin, David Dodd, and Sidney Cottle**    9. *Security Analysis*. New York: McGraw-Hill, 4th ed., 1962.

**Hadley, George**    10. *Nonlinear and Dynamic Programming*. Reading, Mass.: Addison-Wesley, 1964.

**Hicks, J. R.**    11. *Value and Capital*. Oxford: Clarendon Press, 2nd ed., 1946.

**Hirshliefer, J.**    12. "Efficient Allocation of Capital in an Uncertain World," *American Economic Review*, **54** (May 1964), 77–85.

——.    13. "Investment Decision Under Uncertainty—Choice Theoretic Approaches," *The Quarterly Journal of Economics*, **79**, 4 (November 1965), 509–536.

——.    14. "Applications of the State Preference Approach," *The Quarterly Journal of Economics*, **80**, 2 (May 1966), 252–277.

**Lintner, John**    15. "The Valuation of Risk Assets and the Selection of Risky Investments in Stock Portfolios and Capital Budgets," *Review of Economics and Statistics*, February 1965, pp. 394–419.

——.    16. "Security Prices, Risk, and Maximal Gains from Diversification," *Journal of Finance*, December 1965, pp. 587–615.

**Markowitz, Harry M.**    17. "Portfolio Selection," *The Journal of Finance*, March 1952.

——.    18. *Portfolio Selection: Efficient Diversification of Investments*. New York: Wiley, 1959.

| | |
|---|---|
| **Mossin, Jan.** | 19. "Equilibrium in a Capital Asset Market," *Econometrica*, **34**, 4 (October 1966), 768–783. |
| ——. | 20. "Optimal Multi-Period Portfolio Policies," *The Journal of Business*, **41**, 2 (April 1968). |
| **Myers, Stewart C.** | 21. "A Time-State-Preference Model of Security Valuation," *Journal of Financial and Quantitative Analysis*, **3**, 1 (March 1968), 1–34. |
| **Pratt, J. W.** | 22. "Risk Aversion in the Small and in the Large," *Econometrica*, **32**, 1–2 (January-April 1964). |
| **Samuelson, Paul A.** | 23. *Foundations of Economic Analysis*. Cambridge, Mass.: Harvard University Press, 1947. |
| ——. | 24. "Efficient Portfolio Selection for Pareto-Levy Investments," *Journal of Financial and Quantitative Analysis*, (June 1967), pp. 107–121. |
| **Sharpe, William F.** | 25. "A Simplified Model of Portfolio Analysis," *Management Science*, **9**, 2 (January 1963). |
| ——. | 26. "Capital Asset Prices: A Theory of Market Equilibrium under Conditions of Risk," *Journal of Finance*, September 1964, pp. 425–442. |
| ——. | 27. "Security Prices, Risk and Maximal Gains from Diversification: Reply," *Journal of Finance*, December 1966, pp. 743–744. |
| **Tobin, James** | 28. "Liquidity Preference as Behavior Towards Risk," *Review of Economic Studies*, February 1958, pp. 65–86. |
| **von Neumann, John and Oscar Morgenstern** | 29. *Theory of Games and Economic Behavior*. Princeton: Princeton University Press, 3rd ed., 1953. |
| **Williams, John B.** | 30. *The Theory of Investment Value*, Cambridge, Mass.: Harvard University Press, 1938. |
| **Wolf, P.** | 31. "The Simplex Method of Quadratic Programming," *Econometrica*, **27** (1959), 382–398. |

# Index